The Faith of Samuel Johnson

An anthology of his spiritual and moral writings and conversation

CHRISTIAN LIVES

The best way to understand our faith is to see it
lived out in Christian lives, in a variety of settings.
This series aims to supplement Mowbray's col-
lection of biographies by introducing Christian
writers, statesmen and women, church leaders;
people in all walks of life, presented largely in their
own words.

The Faith of
Samuel Johnson

An anthology of his
spiritual and moral writings
and conversation

Presented and edited by
FIONA MACMATH

Line drawings
by E.H. Shepard

MOWBRAY

Mowbray
A Cassell imprint
Villiers House, 41/47 Strand, London WC2N 5JE, England

First published 1990

British Library Cataloguing in Publication Data
Johnson, Samuel, *1709–1784*
    The faith of Samuel Johnson—(Christian lives)
    1. Christian life
    I. Title II. MacMath, Fiona III. Series
    248.4

ISBN 0–264–67195–3

Typeset by Colset Private Limited, Singapore
Printed and bound in Great Britain by
Biddles Ltd, Guildford and King's Lynn

Contents

===

Acknowledgements

The drawings by E.H. Shepard on pp. 11, 14, 28, 36, 42, 56, 68 and 73 are from *Everybody's Boswell*, ed. Frank Morley (G. Bell & Sons, London, 1930) and are reprinted by kind permission of Unwin Hyman Ltd.

The facsimile of Johnson's prayer on p. 101 is reproduced by kind permission of Pembroke College, Oxford.

I would also like to thank all those who have helped me, and without whom this book would not have been written, especially Dr Donald Clarke and Mrs Audrey Sherren of the Princess Helena College, Hitchin, who introduced me to Dr Johnson, and Mr Paul Handley and Mrs Elizabeth Vinten Pinner, who explained how to use a word-processor and microfiche in words of one syllable.

Introduction

Samuel Johnson has become one of those adulated writers whom everyone wishes to have read. There is something decidedly antithetical, however, between the values of his century and ours; few people are attracted to the long eighteenth-century novel, the crafted sermon, the abstruse poetry. A witty bone tossed away by Johnson or Pope is still prized but the meat of eighteenth-century literature is largely the preserve of dismayed undergraduates and a few dedicated professors.

Johnson himself is known as a grand old man of letters, the maker of the first English dictionary, the dogmatic, tea-drinking Tory, famous in his own lifetime. It is still with some wonder that I remember my headmaster, in his farewell speech at the end of one summer term, earnestly recommending James Boswell's *Life of Johnson* to a hundred girls aged between nine and eighteen. In his mind, no doubt, was a cheerful and instructive summer pastime. In theirs were nice calculations about the first possible opportunity to change, undetected, out of school skirts into jeans as tight as a coat of paint. Dr Johnson? – who's he? Few, I fear, responded to the invitation.

Years later, as a staid wife and expectant mother, I found an edition of Boswell, with illustrations by E.H. Shepard. Thinking that Shepard would never have illustrated a dud, I plunged in, breasting the 500 pages of close print and footnotes with ever-increasing enjoyment. (Only 500 pages? It was an abridged edition.)

What I discovered was an entirely different man from the popular image. Behind the gruff lexicographer and lionized conversationalist was a man of unusual humility, charity and Christian faith. Twentieth-century readers might especially identify with his intense depression and fear of death, with which he had to struggle all his life, as well as with his many physical disabilities. His searching and sober assessment of his own shortcomings contrasts with his immense charity towards others, for example the condemned forger, Dr William Dodd, his servants and numerous friends and strangers to whom he gave so generously of his time and money; this though he was never a wealthy man, and constantly reproached himself for idleness.

Small wonder that the young James Boswell adored him! He wrote after his first dinner with him at the Mitre that . . .

> . . . the figure and manner of the celebrated SAMUEL JOHNSON, – the extraordinary power and precision of his conversation, and the pride arising from finding myself admitted as his companion, produced a variety of sensations, and a pleasing elevation of mind, beyond what I had ever before experienced.

This book has arisen because of the enormous influence Johnson has had upon the English-speaking world not only as a man of letters but as a moralist, a deflater of pharisaical cant and a symbol of personal virtue. His worth is perhaps a little overlooked in the late twentieth century, partly through the differences between his time and ours, partly – and more simply – because his writings are difficult to get hold of. Fortunately, though, Boswell's biography has remained in print since its first publication in 1791, six years after Johnson's death, and has secured Johnson's reputation as a deeply religious man – and someone to emulate – far more than Johnson's own writings. Indeed, it is significant that Johnson was extremely diffident about his own qualifications to write on spiritual matters. His *Prayers and Meditations* were for his own private use, or for close friends, and were only prepared for publication at his friends' earnest request. His sermons were all written to be delivered by others, and his diaries were not intended for publication.

But of course Johnson could not hide the depth of his faith; it is evident throughout his 'secular' works. This anthology gives a representative sample of his *Prayers and Meditations* and diary entries. Other writings included are extracts from his essays, sermons, criticism and *Rasselas* (his only novel), and material from his friends, Boswell and Mrs Thrale.

More than most of his contemporaries, he stressed the darker side of Christ's teaching. An easy assurance of salvation by faith was, for him, precluded by his understanding of the parable of the talents. God was never a jolly chum to Johnson, but rather a Father (think how authoritarian and distant an eighteenth-century father was) and a Creator, the Omnipresent and Omnipotent. In many of his meditations, Johnson seems to fear God more than he loves Him; there is a constant sense of guilt, failure and unworthiness.

His extraordinary powers of reasoning and memory added to his sense of failure; the 'genius born to grapple with whole libraries' was always falling short of his own ideals. Throughout his diaries he writes constantly of his struggles against idleness.

Yet his literary output was great, and his health was very poor. Boswell writes:

> In his retrospect on the following Easter-eve, he says, 'When I review the last year, I am able to recollect so little done, that shame and sorrow, though perhaps too weakly, come upon me.' Had he been judging of any one else in the same circumstances, how clear would he have been on the favourable side. How very difficult, and in my opinion almost constitutionally impossible, it was for him to be raised early, even by the strongest resolutions, appears from a note in one of his little paper-books (containing words arranged for his 'Dictionary'), written, I suppose, about 1753: 'I do not remember that, since I left Oxford, I ever rose early by mere choice, but once or twice at Edial, and two or three times for the "Rambler." ' I think he had fair ground enough to have quieted his mind on the subject, by concluding that he was physically incapable of what is at best but a commodious regulation.

As well as having a much more creaturely conception of God than most people today, Johnson shared with his contemporaries an unquestioning belief in absolute moral virtues and a constant interest in discussing them. There were fewer distinctions made between sacred and secular, so that in a periodical like *The Rambler*, Johnson's readers were pleased to consider 'Forgiveness' and 'Self-indulgence' as well as 'Spring' or 'The Benefits of a Garrett' (a light-hearted essay making virtue of the necessity most aspiring writers have of living in attics). Basic Christian belief could be assumed, so that the writer was free to concentrate his energies on developing his ideas on that firm foundation.

Pope's famous definition of wit – 'What oft was thought but ne'er so well expressed' – helps us to understand what writers were setting out to achieve. Originality of thought or plot was not considered a particular virtue, nor was self-expression. Before the Romantic movement, it was considered more worthwhile to make generalizations (now a pejorative word) about the human condition, to present a view of the universe, rather than to dwell on the struggle of the individual. Johnson's sermons are a good example of this; they say nothing startlingly new – but then, what is ever new about the human condition? Their excellence lies in the way Johnson gently but inexorably lays bare the secret self-deceptions that one cherishes about the adequacy of one's response to God. There is no thundering rhetoric or fascinating imagery, merely a polite insistence on rational thought, which leaves the reader smiling but inwardly squirming. He is also particularly sharp when criticizing that trait which is just as common today – that of not thinking about God at all:

> It is astonishing that any man can forbear enquiring seriously, whether there is a God. . . . Let it be remembered, that the nature of things is not alterable by our conduct. We cannot make truth; it is our business only to find it. No proposition can become more or less certain or important, by being considered or rejected.

Johnson and Jane Austen may have belonged to different generations (she was nine when he died) but they share the same restrained but devastating ability to see right to the heart of human folly and expose it with a crisp wit – not through vindictiveness, but as part of their lives' mission to clear away all the rubbish which obscures the goodness of this world.

*

A word should be said about James Boswell, who has written a good part of this book. He could not have had a more different background from Samuel Johnson, being born, not of 'obscure extraction', but the son of the Laird of Auchinleck, an eminent Scottish judge. Boswell read Law and was called to the Bar in Edinburgh in 1766, and in England in 1786. He was thirty-one years younger than Johnson, but much more reactionary, as his *Life* indirectly shows. He was as critical of Johnson's liberal notions about Catholic emancipation and slavery as anyone. He loved London almost as much as the Doctor, and lived as gay and as cosmopolitan a life as was possible until marriage and the duties of his estate kept him at home. Sadly, he was jealous of Johnson's close friendship with Hester Thrale and was not quite as fair to her in the *Life* as he should have been. It was a source of annoyance to him that she enjoyed Johnson's company and trust so exclusively, while he was only able to see him infrequently. To his great delight, he persuaded Johnson to leave 'civilization' and make a tour of Scotland with him. The adventures they had are recorded in his delightful *Journal of a Tour to the Hebrides* published in 1785. The biography of Johnson was written with the Doctor's approval and published in 1791. Boswell outlived his friend by only eleven years; he died in 1795.

Chronology

═══

1709	Samuel Johnson born at Lichfield, 18 September.
1719–25	Studied at Lichfield Grammar School.
1725–26	Studied at Stourbridge Grammar School.
1728	Entered Pembroke College, Oxford, 31 October.
1731	Left college without a degree. Father, Michael Johnson, died.
1732	Taught at Market Bosworth School, Leicestershire.
1735	Published a translation of Father Lobo's *Voyage to Abyssinia*. Married Mrs Elizabeth Porter in Derby, 9 July.
1736	Opened a school in Edial, Staffordshire. (One of the pupils was David Garrick.)
1737	Went to London with Garrick, and began work on a tragedy, *Irene*.
1738	Began to contribute to *The Gentleman's Magazine*. Published *London, a Poem, in Imitation of the Third Satire of Juvenal*.
1744	Published *An Account of the Life of Mr. Richard Savage*.
1745	Published *Miscellaneous Observations on the Tragedy of Macbeth*.
1747	Published *Plan of a Dictionary of the English Language*.
1749	Published *The Vanity of Human Wishes. The Tenth Satire of Juvenal Imitated by Samuel Johnson*. *Irene: A Tragedy* was produced by Garrick at Drury Lane Theatre.
1750–52	Wrote and published *The Rambler*.
1752	His wife died.
1753–54	Wrote essays in *The Adventurer*.
1755	Published *A Dictionary of the English Language*.
1756	Published *Proposals for Printing the Dramatick Works of William Shakespeare*.
1758–60	Wrote and published *The Idler*.

6

1759   His mother died. Published *Rasselas* or *The Prince of Abissinia*.

1762   Received a pension from the King of £300 p.a.

1763   Met James Boswell.

1764   Founded the Literary Club with Sir Joshua Reynolds, Topham Beauclerk, Edmund Burke, Oliver Goldsmith, Bennet Langton, Dr Nugent, Sir John Hawkins and Mr Chamier.

1765   Met Mr and Mrs Henry Thrale. Published *The Plays of William Shakespeare*.

1770   Published *The False Alarm*.

1773   Toured Scotland with Boswell.

1774   Published *The Patriot*.

1775   Granted an honorary degree from Oxford. Published *A Journey to the Western Islands of Scotland* and *Taxation no Tyranny*.
          Went to France with the Thrales.

1779–81   Published *Prefaces, Biographical and Critical, to the Works of the English Poets* (better known as *The Lives of the Poets*).

1784   Died 13 December.

CHAPTER 1
His Character

———

Boswell writes:

And he will be seen as he really was; for I profess to write not his panegyric, which must be all praise, but his life; which, great and good as he was, must not be supposed to be entirely perfect. To be as he was, is indeed subject of panegyric enough to any man in this state of being; but in every picture there should be shade as well as light; and when I delineate him without reserve, I do what he himself recommended, both by his precept and his example.

Samuel Johnson was born at Lichfield, in Staffordshire, on the 18th of September 1709. His father was Michael Johnson, a native of Derbyshire, of obscure extraction, who settled in Lichfield as a bookseller and stationer. His mother was Sarah Ford, descended of an ancient race of substantial yeomanry in Warwickshire. They were well advanced in years when they married, and never had more than two children, both sons; Samuel, their first-born, and Nathaniel, who died in his twenty-fifth year . . .

. . . Johnson's mother was a woman of distinguished understanding. Her piety was not inferior; and to her must be ascribed those early impressions of religion upon the mind of her son, from which the world afterwards derived so much benefit. He told me, that he remembered distinctly having had the first notice of heaven, 'a place to which good people went,' and hell, 'a place to which bad people went,' communicated to him by her, when a little child in bed with her; and that it might be the better fixed in his memory, she sent him to repeat it to Thomas Jackson, their manservant . . .

. . . Of the power of his memory, for which he was all his life eminent to a degree almost incredible, the following early instance was told me. When he was a child in petticoats, and had learnt to read, Mrs. Johnson one morning put the common prayer-book into his hands, pointed to the collect for the day, and said, 'Sam, you must get this by heart.' She went upstairs, leaving him to study it: but by the time she had reached the second floor, she heard him following her. 'What's the matter?' said she. 'I can say it,' he replied; and repeated it distinctly, though he could not have read it more than twice.

. . . Young Johnson had the misfortune to be much afflicted with the scrofula, or king's evil, which disfigured a counte-nance naturally well formed, and hurt his visual nerves so much that he did not see at all with one of his eyes, though its appearance was little different from that of the other. There is amongst his prayers, one inscribed '*When my EYE was restored to its use*,' . . . [but] the force of his attention and perceptive quickness made him see and distinguish all manner of objects with a nicety that is rarely to be found. And the ladies with whom he was acquainted agree, that no man was more nicely and minutely critical in the elegance of female dress . . .

. . . The history of his mind as to religion is an important article. I have mentioned the early impressions made upon his tender imagination by his mother, who continued her pious cares with assiduity, but, in his opinion, not with judgment. 'Sunday,' said he, 'was a heavy day to me when I was a boy. My mother confined me on that day, and made me read "The Whole Duty of Man" from a great part of which I could derive no instruction. I fell into an inattention to religion, or an indifference about it, in my ninth year. The church at Lichfield, in which we had a seat, wanted reparation, so I was to go and find a seat in other churches; and having bad eyes, and being awkward about this, I used to go and read in the fields on Sunday. This habit continued till my fourteenth year; and still I find a great reluctance to go to church. I then became a sort of lax *talker* against religion, for I did not much *think* against it; and this lasted till I went up to Oxford, where it would not be suffered. When at Oxford, I took up Law's *Serious Call to a Holy Life*, expecting to find it a dull book (as such books generally are), and perhaps to laugh at it. But I found Law quite an overmatch for me; and this was the first occasion of my thinking in earnest of religion, after I became capable of rational enquiry.'

*

Boswell remembers his first meeting with Dr Johnson:

He received me very courteously; but it must be confessed, that his apartment, and furniture, and morning dress, were sufficiently uncouth. His brown suit of clothes looked very rusty; he had on a little old shrivelled un-powdered wig, which was too small for his head; his shirt-neck and knees of his breeches were loose; his black worsted stockings ill drawn up; and he had a pair of unbuckled shoes by way of slippers. But all these slovenly particularities were forgotten the moment that he began to talk.

*

Johnson's description of his 'old friend' Sober in an essay on Idleness in The Idler *could easily be a self-mocking portrait. The criticisms it contains he so often levelled at his own head:*

Sober is a man of strong desires and quick imagination, so exactly balanced by the love of ease, that they can seldom stimulate him to any difficult undertaking; they have, how-ever, so much power, that they will not suffer him to lie quite at rest, and though they do not make him sufficiently useful to others, they make him at least weary of himself.

Mr. Sober's chief pleasure is conversation; there is no end of his talk or his attention; to speak or to hear is equally pleasing; for he still fancies that he is teaching or learning something, and is free for the time from his own reproaches.

But there is one time at night when he must go home, that his friends may sleep; and another time in the morning, when

'He received me very courteously.'
Boswell's first meeting with Johnson

all the world agrees to shut out interruption, these are the moments of which poor Sober trembles at the thought. But the misery of these tiresome intervals, he has many means of alleviating. He has persuaded himself that the manual arts are undeservedly overlooked; he has observed in many trades the

11

effects of close thought, and just ratiocination. From specula-
tion he proceeded to practice, and supplied himself with the
tools of a carpenter, with which he mended his coal-box very
successfully, and which he still continues to employ, as he
finds occasion. . . .

Poor Sober! I have often teased him with reproof, and he
has often promised reformation; for no man is so much open
to conviction as the Idler, but there is none on whom it
operates so little. What will be the effect of this paper I know
not; perhaps he will read it and laugh . . . but my hope is that
he will quit his trifles, and betake himself to rational and
useful diligence.

CHAPTER 2
The Women He Loved

═══

Boswell writes:

In a man whom religious education has secured from licentious indulgences, the passion of love, when once it has seized him, is exceedingly strong; being unimpaired by dissipation and totally concentrated in one object. This was experienced by Johnson, when he became the fervent admirer of Mrs. Porter, after her first husband's death. Miss Porter told me, that when he was first introduced to her mother, his appearance was very forbidding: he was then lean and lank, so that his immense structure of bones was hideously striking to the eye, and the scars of the scrofula were deeply visible. He also wore his hair, which was straight and stiff, and separated behind; and he had often had, seemingly, convulsive starts and odd gesticulations, which tended to excite at once surprise and ridicule. Mrs. Porter was so much engaged by his conversation, that she overlooked all these external disadvantages, and said to her daughter,

'This is the most sensible man that I ever saw in my life.'

Though Mrs. Porter was double the age of Johnson, and her person and manner were by no means pleasing to others, she must have had a superiority of understanding and talents, as she certainly inspired him with more than ordinary passion. . . .

'Tetty' died when Johnson was only forty-three and eleven years before he met Boswell. Consequently Boswell can tell us very little about the wife whom Johnson adored, beyond hinting that he thought the match in some way dishonouring to his friend. He was moved, though, by Johnson's obvious grief at the loss – a grief that was to remain part of his life.

13

'His love for his wife was of the
most ardent kind.'
Johnson and Tetty at his school at Edial

The following very solemn and affecting prayer was found after Dr. Johnson's decease, by his servant, Mr. Francis Barber. I present it to the world as an undoubted proof of a circumstance in the character of my illustrious friend, which, though some, whose hard minds I never shall envy, may attack as superstitious, will, I am sure, endear him more to numbers of good men. I have an additional, and that a personal motive for presenting it, because it sanctions what I myself have always maintained and am fond to indulge:

April 26, 1752, being after 12 at night of the 25th O Lord! Governor of heaven and earth, in whose hands are embodied and departed spirits, if thou hast ordained the souls of the dead to minister to the living, and appointed my departed wife to have the care of me, grant that I may enjoy the good effects of her attention and ministration, whether exercised by appearance, impulses, dreams, or in any other manner agreeable to thy government. Forgive my presumption, enlighten my ignorance, and however meaner agents are employed, grant me the blessed influences of thy Holy Spirit, through Jesus Christ our Lord. *Amen.*

That his love for his wife was of the most ardent kind, and, during the long period of fifty years, was unimpaired by the lapse of time, is evident from other memorials, two of which I select, as strongly marking the tenderness and sensibility of his mind.

'MARCH 28, 1753 I kept this day as the anniversary of my Tetty's death, with prayer and tears in the morning, in the evening I prayed for her conditionally, if it were lawful.'

'APRIL 23, 1753 I know not whether I do not too much indulge the vain longings of affection; but I hope they intenerate my heart, and that when I die like my Tetty, this affection will be acknowledged in a happy interview, and that in the meantime I am incited by it to piety. I will, however, not deviate too much from common and received methods of devotion.'

. . . That his sufferings upon the death of his wife were severe, beyond what are commonly endured, I have no doubt, from the information of many who were then about him, to none of whom I give more credit than to Mr. Francis Barber, his faithful negro servant, who came into his family about a fortnight after the dismal event. These sufferings were aggravated by the melancholy inherent in his constitution; and although he probably was not oftener in the wrong than she was, in the little disagreements which sometimes troubled his married state, during which, he owned to me that the gloomy irritability of his existence was more painful to him than ever, he might very naturally, after her death, be tenderly disposed to charge himself with slight omissions and offences, the sense of which would give him much uneasiness.

In 1759, in the month of January, his mother died, at the great age of ninety, an event which deeply affected him; not that 'his mind had acquired no firmness by the contemplation of mortality' [Sir John Hawkins, *Life of Samuel Johnson* (1787), p. 365]; but that his reverential affection for her was not abated by years, as indeed he retained all his tender feelings even to the latest period of his life. I have been told, that he regretted much his not having gone to visit his mother, for several years previous to her death. But he was constantly engaged in literary labours which confined him to London; and though he had not the comfort of seeing his aged parent, he contributed liberally to her support:

TO MRS. JOHNSON, LICHFIELD

13th Jan. 1759

HONOURED MADAM,

The account which Miss [Lucy Porter, his step-daughter] gives me of your health pierces my heart. God comfort and preserve you, for the sake of Jesus Christ.

I would have Miss read to you from time to time the Passion of our Saviour, and sometimes the sentences in the Communion Service, beginning, *Come unto me, all ye that travail and are heavy laden, and I will give you rest.*

I have just now read a physical book, which inclines me to think that a strong infusion of the bark would do you good. Do, dear mother, try it.

Pray, send me your blessing, and forgive all that I have done amiss to you. And whatever you would have done, and what debts you would have paid first, or anything else that you would direct, let Miss [Porter] put it down; I shall endeavour to obey you.

I have got twelve guineas to send you, but unhappily am at a loss how to send it to-night. If I cannot send it to-night, it will come by the next post.

Pray, do not omit any thing mentioned in this letter. God bless you for ever and ever. I am your dutiful son,

SAM. JOHNSON

TO THE SAME

16th Jan. 1795

DEAR HONOURED MOTHER,

Your weakness afflicts me beyond what I am willing to communicate to you. I do not think you unfit to face death, but I know not how to bear the thought of losing you. Endeavour to do all you [can] for yourself. Eat as much as you can.

I pray often for you; do you pray for me. I have nothing to add to my last letter. I am, dear, dear mother, your dutiful son,

SAM. JOHNSON

TO THE SAME

18th Jan. 1759

DEAR HONOURED MOTHER,

I fear you are too ill for long letters; therefore I will only tell you, you have from me all the regard that can possibly subsist in the heart. I pray God to bless you for evermore, for Jesu Christ's sake. Amen.

Let Miss write to me every post, however short.

I am, dear mother, your dutiful son,

SAM. JOHNSON

TO MISS PORTER, AT MRS. JOHNSON'S, IN LICHFIELD

20th Jan. 1759

DEAR MISS,

I will, if it be possible, come down to you. God grant I may yet [find] my dear mother breathing and sensible. Do not tell her lest I disappoint her. If I miss to write next post, I am on the road. I am my dearest Miss, your most humble servant.

SAM. JOHNSON

On the other side:

20th Jan. 1759

DEAR HONOURED MOTHER,

Neither your condition nor your character make it fit for me to say much. You have been the best mother, and I believe the best woman in the world. I thank you for your indulgence to me, and beg forgiveness of all that I have done ill, and all that I have omitted to do well. God grant you his Holy Spirit, and receive you to everlasting happiness, for Jesus Christ's sake. Amen. Lord Jesus receive your spirit. Amen, – I am, dear, dear mother, your dutiful son,

SAM. JOHNSON

TO MISS PORTER, IN LICHFIELD

23rd Jan. 1759

You will conceive my sorrow for the loss of my mother, of the best mother. If she were to live again, surely I should behave better to her. But she is happy, and what is past is nothing to her; and for me, since I cannot repair my faults to her, I hope repentance will efface them. I return you and all those that have been good to her my sincerest thanks, and pray God to repay you all with infinite advantage. Write to me, and comfort me, dear child. I shall be glad likewise, if Kitty will write to me. I shall send a bill of twenty pounds in a few days, which I thought to have brought to my mother; but God suffered it not. I have not power or composure to say much more. God bless you, and bless us all. I am, dear Miss, your affectionate humble servant,

SAM. JOHNSON

Something should be said about the third woman Johnson loved,
because it was largely due to her efforts that Johnson knew any
happiness and relief from his exacting conscience. Boswell writes:

Mr. Thrale [a wealthy brewer] had married Miss Hester
Lynch Salusbury, of good Welsh extraction, a lady of lively
talents, improved by education. Johnson accepted of an
invitation to dinner at Thrale's, and was so much pleased with
his reception, both by Mr. and Mrs. Thrale, and they so much
pleased with him, that his invitations to their house were more
and more frequent, till at last he became one of the family, and
an apartment was appropriated to him, both in their house at
Southwark and in their villa at Streatham.

*

As Boswell said, Johnson received much kindness from the Thrale
family. What he does not say is that Johnson had lived for part of
every week with the Thrales, becoming a very close member of their
family for many years. During that time, Hester Thrale had lavished
her high spirits and solicitude upon him, especially during his
periods of depression. Less well-known is the fact that Johnson
helped her greatly when Mr Thrale's health and spirits failed and the
brewery ran into grave financial difficulties. Together, they sorted
out Thrale's affairs and finally set the business up in new hands,
leaving Mrs Thrale and her daughters reasonably provided for.

Sadly, from the time of Mr Thrale's death, there was an estrange-
ment between Mrs Thrale and Johnson. Hester had devoted herself
to her family, her husband – not an easy man – and Johnson for
many years. She fell in love with her daughter's Italian music
teacher, and, much to her family's and Johnson's disapproval, even-
tually married him. Boswell, who one suspects was always jealous of
Mrs Thrale, is at his most cutting, ascribing her love-match to the
fact that 'the manly authority of the husband no longer curbed the
lively exuberance of the lady.' Certainly Johnson was very affected
by the switch of her attention away from himself and there survives a
prayer which he composed on leaving the Thrale household:

Almighty God, Father of all mercy, help me by thy grace, that
I may, with humble and sincere thankfulness, remember the
comforts and conveniences which I have enjoyed at this place;
and that I may resign them with holy submission, equally

trusting in thy protection when thou givest and when thou takest away. Have mercy upon me, O Lord! have mercy upon me!

To thy fatherly protection, O Lord, I commend this family. Bless, guide, and defend them, that they may so pass through this world, as finally to enjoy in thy presence everlasting happiness, for Jesus Christ's sake. Amen.

Boswell adds:

One cannot read this prayer without some emotions not very favourable to the lady whose conduct occasioned it.

*

On a happier note, we have a picture of the three of them at the beginning of their friendship:

Being informed that he was at Mr. Thrale's in the Borough, I hastened thither, and found Mrs. Thrale and him at breakfast. I was kindly welcomed. In a moment he was in a full glow of conversation, and I felt myself elevated as if brought into another state of being. Mrs. Thrale and I looked to each other while we talked, and our looks expressed our congenial admiration and affection for him. I shall ever recollect this scene with great pleasure. I exclaimed to her, 'I am now intellectually, *Hermippus redivivus*; I am quite restored by him, by transfusion of mind.' 'There are many,' she replied, 'who admire and respect Mr. Johnson; but you and I *love* him.'

*

Another characteristic picture of him is given in Mrs Thrale's memoirs:

Dr. Johnson loved late hours extremely, or, more properly, hated early ones. Nothing was more terrifying to him than the idea of retiring to bed, which he never would call going to rest, or suffer another to call so. 'I lie down,' said he, 'that my acquaintance may sleep; but I lie down to endure oppressive misery, and soon to rise again to pass the night in anxiety and pain.' By this pathetic manner, which no one ever possessed in so eminent a degree, he used to shock me from quitting his company, till I hurt my own health not a little by sitting up with him when I was myself far from well; nor was it an easy matter to oblige him even by compliance, for he always maintained that no one forbore their own gratifications for the sake of pleasing another, and if one *did* sit up, it was probably to amuse one's self. Some right, however, he certainly had to say so, as he made his company exceedingly entertaining when he had once forced one, by his vehement lamentations and piercing reproofs, not to quit the room, but to sit quietly and make tea for him, as I often did in London till four o'clock in the morning. At Streatham I managed better, having always some friend who was kind enough to engage him in talk, and favour my retreat: and he rose in the morning as unwillingly as he went to bed.

She was obviously good for him, keeping the melancholy at bay with her wit and astringent good sense. It is interesting to learn that the late rising which he so much reproaches himself with was not entirely occasioned by illness. It might be that his depression and insomnia fed upon each other, which made going to bed a hateful prospect to him. The next chapter will deal with his depression, the lifting of which was due so much to the kindness and affection of the Thrales.

CHAPTER 3

His Morbid Melancholy

All his life, Johnson seems to have battled against depression. Boswell describes his first bout of severe depression when he was still a student:

The 'morbid melancholy,' which was lurking in his constitution, and to which we may ascribe those particularities, and that aversion to regular life, which at a very early period marked his character, gathered such strength in his twentieth year, as to afflict him in a dreadful manner. While he was at Lichfield, in the college vacation of the year 1729, he felt himself overwhelmed with a horrible hypochondria, with perpetual irritation, fretfulness, and impatience; and with a dejection, gloom, and despair, which made existence misery. He was sometimes so languid and inefficient, that he could not distinguish the hour upon the town clock.

Johnson, upon the first violent attack of this disorder, strove to overcome it by forcible exertions. He frequently walked to Birmingham and back again, and tried many other expedients, but all in vain. His expression concerning it to me was, 'I did not then know how to manage it.' His distress became so intolerable, that he applied to Dr. Swinfen, physician in Lichfield, his godfather, and put into his hands a state of his case, written in Latin.

*

Like many sensitive people, Johnson's emotions were intense and contradictory. He loved nothing better than an exhilarating drive with a pretty young lady by his side, or a night on the town with his friends. But the other side of this was a deep sense of guilt and failure, and a dread of death. This was, no doubt, worsened by all his physical disabilities. Ill health naturally breeds hypochondria, and belief in an exacting Creator breeds guilt and fear. His diary for Easter Eve, 1761 reads:

Since the Communion of last Easter I have led a life so dissipated and useless, and my terrors and perplexities have so much increased, that I am under great depression and discouragement, yet I purpose to present myself before God tomorrow with humble hope that he will not break the bruised reed.

Come unto me all ye that travail.

I have resolved, I hope not presumptuously, till I am afraid to resolve again. Yet hoping in God I steadfastly purpose to lead a new life. O God, enable me, for Jesus Christ's sake.

My Purpose is
1 [obliterated]
2 To avoid Idleness.
   To regulate my sleep as to length and choice of hours.
   To set down every day what shall be done the day following.
   To keep a Journal.
3 To worship God more diligently.
   To go to Church every Sunday.
4 To study the Scriptures.
   To read a certain portion every week.

Almighty and most merciful Father look down upon my misery with pity, strengthen me that I may overcome all sinful habits, grant that I may with effectual faith commemorate the death of thy son Jesus Christ, so that all corrupt desires may be extinguished, and all vain thoughts may be dispelled. Enlighten me with true knowledge, animate me with reasonable hope, comfort me with a just sense of thy love, and assist me to the performance of all holy purposes, that after the sins, errors, and miseries of this world I may obtain everlasting happiness for Jesus Christ's sake. To whom &c. Amen.

I hope to attend on God in his ordinances to morrow. Trust in God O my soul. O God let me trust in Thee.

*

Boswell gives us his diary entry for Easter 1764:

In this year, except what he may have done in revising Shakespeare, we do not find that Johnson laboured much in literature. The ease and independence to which he had at last attained by royal munificence, increased his natural indolence. In his 'Meditations,' he thus accuses himself:

'GOOD FRIDAY, APRIL 20, 1764. I have made no reformation; I have lived totally useless, more sensual in thought, and more addicted to wine and meat.'

He then solemnly says, 'This is not the life to which heaven is promised'; and he earnestly resolves an amendment.

It was his custom to observe certain days with a pious abstraction: viz., New Year's Day, the day of his wife's death, Good Friday, Easter Day, and his own birthday. He this year says,

'I have now spent fifty-five years in resolving; having, from the earliest time almost that I can remember, been forming schemes of a better life. I have done nothing. The need of doing, therefore, is pressing, since the time of doing is short. O God, grant me to resolve aright, and to keep my resolutions, for Jesus Christ's sake. Amen.'

Such a tenderness of conscience, such a fervent desire of improvement, will rarely be found. . . .

About this time he was afflicted with a very severe return of the hypochondriac disorder, which was ever lurking about him. He was so ill, as, not withstanding his remarkable love of company, to be entirely averse to society, the most fatal symptom of that malady. Dr. Adams told me, that, as an old friend, he was admitted to visit him, and that he found him in a deplorable state, sighing, groaning, talking to himself, and restlessly walking from room to room. He then used this emphatical expression of the misery which he felt: 'I would consent to have a limb amputated to recover my spirits.'

Talking to himself was, indeed, one of his singularities ever since I knew him. I was certain that he was frequently uttering pious ejaculations; for fragments of the Lord's Prayer have been distinctly overheard. . . .

*

In the next year, Johnson writes again of his fear and failure:

EASTER DAY, APR. 7, 1765 ABOUT 3 IN THE MORNING. I purpose again to partake of the blessed Sacrament, yet when I consider how vainly I have hitherto resolved at this annual commemoration of my Saviour's death to regulate my life by his laws, I am almost afraid to renew my resolutions. Since the last Easter I have reformed no evil habit, my time has been unprofitably spent, and seems as a dream that has left nothing behind. My memory grows confused, and I know not how the days pass over me.

Good Lord deliver me.

I will call upon God tomorrow for repentance and amendment. O heavenly Father let not my call be vain, but grant me to desire what may please thee, and fulfill those desires for Jesus Christ's sake. Amen.

My resolutions, which God perfect, are:

1 To avoid loose thoughts
2 [obliterated]
3 To rise at eight every morning.

I hope to extend these purposes to other duties, but it is necessary to combat evil habits singly. I purpose to rise at eight because though I shall not yet rise early it will be much earlier than I now rise, for I often lie till two, and will gain me much time, and tend to a conquest over idleness and give time for other duties. I hope to rise yet earlier.

Almighty and most merciful Father, who hatest nothing that thou hast made, nor desirest the Death of a Sinner, look down with mercy upon me, and grant that I may turn from my wickedness and live. Forgive the days and years which I have passed in folly, idleness, and sin. Fill me with such sorrow for the time misspent, that I may amend my life according to thy holy word, strengthen me against habitual idleness and enable me to direct my thoughts to the performance of my duty: that while I live I may serve thee in the state to which thou shalt call me, and at last by a holy and happy death be delivered from the struggles, and sorrows of this life, and obtain eternal happiness by thy mercy, for the sake of Jesus Christ our Lord. Amen.

O God, have mercy on me.

At church I purpose:

Before I leave the pew to pray the occasional prayer, and read my resolutions

To pray for Tetty and the rest; the like after Communion.

At intervals to use the collects of fourth after Trinity, and first and fourth after Epiph. and to meditate.

SEPT. 18, 1768 AT NIGHT. Townmalling in Kent.

I have now begun the sixtieth year of my life. How the last year has past I am unwilling to terrify myself with thinking. This day has been past in great perturbation. I was distracted at Church in an uncommon degree, and my distress has had very little intermission. I have found myself somewhat relieved by reading, which I therefore intend to practise when I am able. This day it came into my mind to write the history of my melancholy. On this I purpose to deliberate. I know not whether it may not too much disturb me.

*

Much later, in 1780, Boswell wrote to Johnson about his own melancholy. Johnson was struggling to preserve his own equilibrium for Henry Thrale had suffered a second stroke and Topham Beauclerk, an old friend, had died at the age of forty. His rather tart reply sheds light on his own way of 'managing':

'You are always complaining of melancholy, and I conclude from those complaints that you are fond of it. No man talks of that which he is desirous to conceal, and every man desires to conceal that of which he is ashamed. . . . Make it an invariable and obligatory law to yourself, never to mention your own mental diseases; if you are never to speak of them, you will think on them but little, and if you think little of them, they will molest you rarely. When you talk of them, it is plain that you want either praise or pity; for praise there is no room, and pity will do you no good.'

*

In 1772 Boswell writes:

At this time, it appears, from his 'Prayers and Meditations,' that he had been more than commonly diligent in religious duties, particularly in reading the Holy Scriptures. It was Passion Week, that solemn season which the Christian world has appropriated to the commemoration of the mysteries of our redemption, and during which, whatever embers of religion are in our breasts, will be kindled into pious warmth.

I paid him short visits both on Friday and Saturday; and, seeing his large folio Greek Testament before him, beheld him with a reverential awe, and would not intrude upon his time. While he was thus employed to such good purpose, and while his friends in their intercourse with him constantly found a vigorous intellect and a lively imagination, it is melancholy to read in his private register, 'My mind is unsettled and my memory confused. I have of late turned my thoughts with a very useless earnestness upon past incidents. I have yet got no command over my thoughts: an unpleasing incident is almost certain to hinder my rest.'

*

Perhaps the following is a fairer assessment of his failings than Johnson was ever able to make formerly. It is good to read that he did receive some comfort, as well as conviction of sin, from his worship.

EASTER DAY, 1776, APR. 7. The time is again at which, since the death of my poor dear Tetty, on whom God have mercy, I have annually commemorated the mystery of Redemption, and annually purposed to amend my life. My reigning sin, to which perhaps many others are appendent, is waste of time, and general sluggishness, to which I was always inclined and in part of my life have been almost compelled by morbid melancholy and disturbance of mind. Melancholy has had me in its paroxisms and remissions, but I have not improved the intervals, nor sufficiently resisted my natural inclination, or sickly habits. I will resolve henceforth to rise at eight in the morning, so far as resolution is proper, and will pray that God will strengthen me. I have begun this morning.

Johnson 'resists his natural inclination' and puts
his books in order

Though for the past week I have had an anxious design of communicating to day, I performed no particular act of devotion, till on Friday I went to Church. My design was to pass parts of the day in exercises of piety but Mr. Boswell interrupted me; of him however I could have rid myself, but poor Thrale, *orbus et exspes* [bereft and hopeless – he had recently lost his seventh child, the last remaining son], came for comfort and sat till seven when we all went to Church.

In the morning I had at Church some radiations of comfort . . .

*

Boswell writes:

In 1777, it appears from his 'Prayers and Meditations' that Johnson suffered much from a state of mind 'unsettled and perplexed', and from that constitutional gloom which, together with his extreme humility and anxiety with regard to his religious state, made him contemplate himself through too dark and unfavourable a medium. It may be said of him, that he 'saw God in clouds.' Certain we may be of his injustice to himself in the following lamentable paragraph:

'When I survey my past life, I discover nothing but a barren waste of time, with some disorders of body, and disturbances of the mind very near to madness, which I hope He that made me will suffer to extenuate many faults, and excuse many deficiencies.'

*

At the age of seventy-two, most people are either content with themselves, or see no hope of ever changing their lives. But Johnson's faith was still vital and would allow no complacency. Moreover, he was not, unlike many elderly people, apt to blame others for his own missed opportunities. He retained a clear sense of his own failure and guilt – perhaps too much so – until his death.

EASTER EVE, APR. 14, 1781 On Good Friday I took in the Afternoon some coffee and buttered cake, and today I had a little bread at breakfast, and potatoes and apples in the afternoon, the tea with a little toast, but I find myself feeble and unsustained, and suspect that I can not bear to fast so long as formerly.

This day I read some of Clarke's Sermons. [Dr Samuel Clarke 1675–1729.]

I hope that since my last Communion I have advanced by pious reflections in my submission to God, and my benevolence to Man, but I have corrected no external habits, nor have kept any of the resolutions made in the beginning of the year, yet I hope still to be reformed, and not to lose my whole life in idle purposes. Many years are already gone, irrevocably passed in useless Misery; that what remains may be spent better, grant O God.

Nevertheless, this is a heartening little note which he wrote towards the end of his life.

SEPT. 18, 1781. This is my seventy third birthday an awful day. I said a preparatory prayer last night, and waking early made use in the dark, as I sat up in bed of the prayer (beginning of this year). I rose, breakfasted and gave thanks at Church for my Creation, Preservation, and Redemption. As I came home I thought I had never begun any period of life so placidly. I read the second Epistle to the Thessalonians, and looked into Hammond's notes. I have always accustomed to let this day pass unnoticed, but it came this time into my [mind] that some little festivity was not improper. I had a Dinner and invited Allen and Levet.

CHAPTER 4

On Death

===

From an essay in The Idler, *No. 41, Saturday, 27 January 1759:*

We know little of the state of departed souls, because such knowledge is not necessary to a good life. Reason deserts us at the brink of the grave, and can give no further intelligence. Revelation is not wholly silent. *There is joy in the Angels of Heaven over one Sinner that repenteth*; and surely this joy is not incommunicable to souls disentangled from the body, and made like Angels.

Let Hope therefore dictate, what Revelation does not confute, that the union of souls may still remain; and that we who are struggling with sin, sorrow, and infirmities, may have our part in the attention and kindness of those who have finished their course, and are now receiving their reward.

*

Boswell records the following conversation which he had with Johnson in 1772:

I again visited him at night. Finding him in a very good humour, I ventured to lead him to the subject of our situation in a future state, having much curiosity to know his notions on that point. JOHNSON: 'Why, Sir, the happiness of an unembodied spirit will consist in a consciousness of the favour of God, in the contemplation of truth, and in the possession of felicitating ideas.' BOSWELL: 'But, Sir, is there any harm in our forming to ourselves conjectures as to the particulars of our happiness, though the Scripture has said but very little on the subject? "We know not what we shall be." ' JOHNSON: 'Sir, there is no harm. What philosophy suggests to us to this topic is probable: what Scripture tells us is certain. Dr. Henry More has carried it as far as philosophy can. You may buy both his theological and philosophical works, in two volumes folio, for about eight shillings.' BOSWELL: 'One of the most pleasing thoughts is, that we shall see our friends again.' JOHNSON: 'Yes, Sir: but you must consider, that when we are become purely rational, many of our friendships will be cut off. Many friendships are formed by a community of sensual pleasures: all these will be cut off. We form many friendships with bad men, because they have agreeable qualities, and they can be useful to us; but, after death, they can no longer be of use to us. We form many friendships by mistake, imagining people to be different from what they really are. After death, we shall see every one in a true light. Then, Sir, they talk of our meeting our relations; but then all relationship is dissolved; and we shall have no regard for one person more than another, but for their real value. However, we shall either have the satisfaction of meeting our friends, or be satisfied without meeting them.' BOSWELL: 'Yet Sir, we see in Scripture, that Dives still retained an anxious concern about his brethren.' JOHNSON: 'Why, Sir, we must either suppose that passage to be metaphorical, or hold, with many divines and all the Purgatorians, that departed souls do not all at once arrive at the utmost perfection of which they are capable.' BOSWELL: 'I think, Sir, that is a very rational supposition.' JOHNSON: 'Why yes, Sir; but we do not know it is a true one. There is no harm in believing it; but you must not compel others to make it an article of faith; for it is not revealed.' . . .

*

Five years later, he and Johnson spoke again on the same subject:

While Johnson and I stood in calm conference by ourselves in Dr. Taylor's garden, at a pretty late hour in a serene autumn night, looking up to the heavens, I directed the discourse to the subject of a future state. My friend was in a placid and most benignant frame of mind. 'Sir,' said he, 'I do not imagine that all things will be made clear to us immediately after death, but that the ways of Providence will be explained to us very gradually.' I ventured to ask him whether, although the words of some texts of Scripture seemed strong in support of the dreadful doctrine of an eternity of punishment, we might not hope that the denunciation was figurative, and would not literally be executed. JOHNSON: 'Sir, you are to consider the intention of punishment in a future state. We have no reason to be sure that we shall then be no longer liable to offend against God. We do not know that even the angels are quite in a state of security; nay, we know that some of them have fallen. It may therefore, perhaps, be necessary, in order to preserve both men and angels in a state of rectitude, that they should have continually before them the punishment of those who have deviated from it; but we hope that by some other means a fall from rectitude may be prevented. Some of the texts of Scripture upon this subject are, as you observe, indeed strong; but they may admit of a mitigated interpretation.' He talked to me upon this awful and delicate question in a gentle tone, and as if afraid to be decisive.

*

Johnson's fear of death was marvelled at by his contemporaries; they expected such a faithful Christian and learned philosopher to have, perhaps, more resolution and courage in the face of the inevitable. Or perhaps, as Johnson conjectures, the majority of them were too dull or apathetic to consider seriously its implications. The following extract is from the last edition of The Idler *and it explores the sadness of change and mortality.*

Much of the Pain and Pleasure of mankind arises from the conjectures which every one makes of the thoughts of others; we all enjoy praise which we do not hear, and resent contempt which we do not see. The *Idler* may therefore be forgiven, if he suffers his Imagination to represent to him what his readers will say or think when they are informed that they have now his last paper in their hands.

Value is more frequently raised by scarcity than by use. That which lay neglected when it was common, rises in estimation as its quantity becomes less. We seldom learn the true want of what we have till it is discovered that we can have no more.

This essay will, perhaps, be read with care even by those who have not yet attended to any other; and he that finds this late attention recompensed, will not forbear to wish that he had bestowed it sooner.

Though the *Idler* and his readers have contracted no close friendship, they are perhaps both unwilling to part. There are few things not purely evil, of which we can say, without some emotion of uneasiness, *this is the last*. Those who never could agree together, shed tears when mutual discontent has determined them to final separation; of a place which has been frequently visited, tho' without pleasure, the last look is taken with heaviness of heart; and the *Idler*, with all his chillness of tranquillity, is not wholly unaffected by the thought that his last essay is now before him.

This secret horror of the last is inseparable from a thinking being whose life is limited, and to whom death is dreadful. We always make a secret comparison between a part and the whole; the termination of any period of life reminds us that life itself has likewise its termination; when we have done any thing for the last time, we involuntarily reflect that a part of the days allotted to us is past, and that as more is past there is less remaining.

It is very happily and kindly provided, that in every life there are certain pauses and interruptions, which force consideration upon the careless, and seriousness upon the light; points of time where one course of action ends and another begins: and by vicissitude of fortune, or alteration of employment, by change of place, or loss of friendship, we are forced to say of something, *this is the last*.

An even and unvaried tenor of life always hides from our apprehension the approach of its end. Succession is not perceived but by variation; he that lives today as he lived yesterday, and expects that, as the present day is such will be the morrow, easily conceives time as running in a circle and returning to itself. The uncertainty of our duration is impressed commonly by dissimilitude of condition; it is only by finding life changeable that we are reminded of its shortness.

This conviction, however forcible at every new impression, is every moment fading from the mind; and partly by the inevitable incursion of new images, and partly by voluntary exclusion of unwelcome thoughts, we are again exposed to the universal fallacy; and we must do another thing for the last time, before we consider that the time is nigh when we shall do no more.

As the last *Idler* is published in that solemn week which the Christian world has always set apart for the examination of the conscience, the review of life, the extinction of earthly desires and the renovation of holy purposes, I hope that my readers are already disposed to view every incident with seriousness, and improve it by meditation; and that when they see this series of trifles brought to a conclusion, they will consider that by outliving the *Idler*, they have passed weeks, months, and years which are now no longer in their power; that an end must in time be put to every thing great as to every thing little; that to life must come its last hour, and to this system of being its last day, the hour at which probation ceases, and repentance will be vain; the day in which every work of the hand, and imagination of the heart shall be brought to judgment, and an everlasting futurity shall be determined by the past.

*

Boswell records the following exchanges in 1769:

I mentioned to him that I had seen the execution of several convicts at Tyburn two days before, and that none of them seemed to be under any concern. JOHNSON: 'Most of them, Sir, have never thought at all.' BOSWELL: 'But is not the fear of death natural to man?' JOHNSON: 'So much so, Sir, that the whole of life is but keeping away the thoughts of it.' He then, in a low and earnest tone, talked of his meditating upon the awful hour of his own dissolution, and in what manner he should conduct himself upon that occasion: 'I know not,' said

'His mind resembled the vast amphitheatre, the Coliseum at Rome.'

Johnson's daily submission to a freshly ordered wig

he, 'whether I should wish to have a friend by me, or have it all between God and myself.'

When we were alone, I introduced the subject of death, and endeavoured to maintain that the fear of it might be got over. I told him that David Hume said to me, he was no more uneasy to think he should *not be* after this life, than that he *had not been* before he began to exist. JOHNSON: 'Sir, if he really thinks so, his perceptions are disturbed; he is mad: if he does not think so, he lies. He may tell you, he holds his finger in the flame of a candle without feeling pain; would you believe him? When he dies, he at least gives up all he has.' BOSWELL: 'Foote, Sir, told me, that when he was very ill he was not afraid to die.' JOHNSON: 'It is not true, Sir. Hold a pistol to Foote's breast, or to Hume's breast, and threaten to kill them; and you'll see how they behave.' BOSWELL: 'But may we not fortify our minds for the approach of death?' Here I am sensible I was in the wrong, to bring before his view what he ever looked upon with horror; for although, when in a celestial frame of mind, in his *Vanity of Human Wishes*, he has supposed death to be 'kind Nature's signal for retreat' from this state of being to 'a happier seat,' his thoughts upon this awful change were in general full of dismal apprehensions. His mind resembled the vast amphitheatre, the Coliseum at Rome. In the centre stood his judgment, which, like a mighty gladiator, combated those apprehensions that, like the wild beasts of the *arena*, were all around in cells, ready to be let out upon him. After a conflict he drives them back into their dens; but not killing them, they were still assailing him. To my question, whether we might not fortify our minds for the approach of death, he answered, in a passion, 'No, Sir, let it alone. It matters not how a man dies, but how he lives. The act of dying is not of importance, it lasts so short a time.' He added (with an earnest look), 'A man knows it must be so, and submits. It will do him no good to whine.' . . .

*

His birthday meditation and prayer four years later show that fear which many people share, of failing to use wisely such talents as they have been given.

TALISKER IN SKYE, SEPT. 24, 1773. On last Saturday was my sixty fourth Birthday. I might perhaps have forgotten it had not Boswell told me of it, and, what pleased me less, told the family at Dunvegan.

The last year is added to those of which little use has been made. I tried in the Summer to learn Dutch, and was inter-rupted by an inflammation in my eye. I set out in August on this Journey to Skye. I find my memory uncertain, but hope it is only by a life immethodical and scattered. Of my Body I do not perceive that exercise or change of air has yet either increased the strength or activity. My Nights are still dis-turbed by flatulencies.

My hope is, for resolution I dare no longer call it, to divide my time regularly, and to keep such a journal of my time, as may give me comfort in reviewing it. But when I consider my age, and the broken state of my body, I have great reason to fear lest Death should lay hold upon me, while I am yet only designing to live. But, I have yet hope.

Almighty God, most merciful Father, look down upon me with pity; thou hast protected me in childhood and youth, support me, Lord, in my declining years. Deliver me from evil thoughts and scruples and preserve me from the dangers of sinful presumption. Give me, if it be best for me, stability of purposes, and tranquillity of mind. Let the year which I have now begun, be spent to thy glory, and to the furtherance of my salvation. Take not from me thy holy Spirit, but as Death approaches, prepare me to appear joyfully in thy presence for the sake of Jesus Christ our Lord. Amen.

*

Johnson's only novel, Rasselas, *explores one of his major themes, the vanity of human wishes in the face of certain and imminent death. In the final pages, Imlac, the philosopher, and the Prince and Princess of Abyssinia visit the catacombs in Egypt:*

'But the Being,' said Nekayah, 'whom I fear to name, the Being which made the soul, can destroy it.'

'He, surely, can destroy it,' answered Imlac, 'since, however unperishable, it receives from a superior nature its power of duration. That it will not perish by any inherent cause of decay, or principle of corruption, may be shown by philosophy; but philosophy can tell no more. That it will not be annihilated by him that made it, we must humbly learn from higher authority.'

The whole assembly stood a while silent and collected. 'Let us return,' said Rasselas, 'from this scene of mortality. How gloomy would be these mansions of the dead to him who did not know that he shall never die; that what now acts will continue its agency, and what now thinks shall think on for ever. Those that lie here stretched before us, the wise and the powerful of ancient times, warn us to remember the shortness of our present state: they were, perhaps, snatched away while they were busy, like us, in the choice of life.'

'To me,' said the princess, 'the choice of life is become less important; I hope hereafter to think only on the choice of eternity.'

*

In his last year, Johnson and Boswell went to stay in Oxford with his old friend, Dr William Adams, Master of Pembroke, Johnson's old College.

Dr. Johnson surprised him not a little, by acknowledging with a look of horror, that he was much oppressed by the fear of death. The amiable Dr. Adams suggested that God was infinitely good. JOHNSON: 'That he is infinitely good, as far as the perfection of his nature will allow, I certainly believe; but it is necessary for good upon the whole, that individuals should be punished. As to an *individual*, therefore, he is not infinitely good; and as I cannot be *sure* that I have fulfilled the conditions on which salvation is granted, I am afraid I may be one of those who shall be damned.' (Looking dismally.) DR. ADAMS: 'What do you mean by damned?' JOHNSON

39

(passionately and loudly): 'Sent to hell, Sir, and punished everlastingly.' DR. ADAMS: 'I don't believe that doctrine.' JOHNSON: 'Hold, Sir: do you believe that some will be punished at all?' DR. ADAMS: 'Being excluded from heaven will be a punishment; yet there may be no great positive suffering.' JOHNSON: 'Well, Sir, but if you admit of any degree of punishment, there is an end of your argument for infinite goodness simply considered; for infinite goodness would inflict no punishment whatever. There is not infinite goodness physically considered: morally there is.' BOSWELL: 'But may not a man attain to such a degree of hope as not to be uneasy from the fear of death?' JOHNSON: 'A man may have such a degree of hope as to keep him quiet. You see I am not quiet, from the vehemence with which I talk; but I do not despair.' MRS. ADAMS: 'You seem, Sir, to forget the merits of our Redeemer.' JOHNSON: 'Madam, I do not forget the merits of my Redeemer; but my Redeemer has said that he will set some on his right hand and some on his left.' – He was in gloomy agitation, and said, 'I'll have no more on't.'

CHAPTER 5

His Search for the Truth

===

From a sermon on the text: 'Knowing this first, that there shall come in the last days scoffers, walking after their own lusts.' (II Peter iii.3)

It is astonishing that any man can forbear enquiring seriously, whether there is a God; whether God is just; whether this life is the only state of existence; whether God has appointed rewards and punishments in a future state; whether he has given any laws for the regulation of our conduct here; whether he has given them by revelation; and whether the religion publicly taught carries any mark of divine appointment. These are questions which every reasonable being ought undoubtedly to consider with an attention suitable to their importance; and he, whom the consideration of eternal happiness or misery cannot awaken from his pleasing dreams, cannot prevail upon to suspend his mirth, surely ought not to despise others for dullness and stupidity.

Let it be remembered, that the nature of things is not alterable by our conduct. We cannot make truth; it is our business only to find it. No proposition can become more or less certain or important, by being considered or neglected. It is to no purpose to wish, or to suppose, that to be false, which is in itself true, and therefore to acquiesce in our own wishes and suppositions, when the matter is of eternal consequence, to believe obstinately without grounds of belief, and to determine without examination, is the last degree of folly and absurdity. It is not impossible that he who acts in this manner may obtain the approbation of madmen like himself, but he will incur the contempt of every wise man; and, what is more to be feared, amidst his security and supineness, his sallies and his flights, 'He that sitteth in the heavens shall laugh him to scorn; the Lord shall have him in derision.' (see Psalm ii.4)

The advances in science which led to new philosophical and reli-
gious ideas influenced Christians as much as freethinkers. To
Johnson rational thought and action demanded increased study of
Scripture, faith and penitence, rather than a forsaking of old truths.
Apathy on this all-important subject was as intellectually unten-
able as, or more so than, atheism. But to Johnson, atheism was never
an acceptable position. Boswell comments on the difference between
his friend and Voltaire:

Voltaire's *Candide*, written to refute the system of Optimism,
which it has accomplished with brilliant success, is wonder-
fully similar in its plan and conduct to Johnson's *Rasselas*; . . .
Though the proposition illustrated by both these works was
the same, namely, that in our present state there is more evil
than good, the intention of the writers was very different.
Voltaire, I am afraid, meant only by wanton profaneness to
obtain a sportive victory over religion, and to discredit the

The Literary Club. *From left to right:* Langton, Gibbon, Percy,
Reynolds, Johnson, Steevens (*foreground*), Boswell, Chamier

belief of a superintending Providence: Johnson meant, by showing the unsatisfactory nature of things temporal, to direct the hopes of man to things eternal.

And he records the following defence of the truth of Christianity:

Talking of those who denied the truth of Christianity, he [Johnson] said, 'It is always easy to be on the negative side. If a man were now to deny that there is salt upon the table, you could not reduce him to an absurdity. Come, let us try this a little further. I deny that Canada is taken, and I can support my denial by pretty good arguments. The French are a much more numerous people than we; and it is not likely that they would allow us to take it. "But the ministry have assured us, in all the formality of the 'Gazette,' that it is taken." – Very true. But the ministry have put us to an enormous expense by the war in America, and it is their interest to persuade us that we have got something for our money. – "But the fact is confirmed by thousands of men who were at the taking of it." – Ay, but these men have still more interest in deceiving us. They don't want that you should think the French have beat them, but that they have beat the French. Now suppose you should go over and find that it really is taken; that would only satisfy yourself; for when you come home we will not believe you. We will say, you have been bribed. – Yet, Sir, notwithstanding all these plausible objections, we have no doubt that Canada is really ours. Such is the weight of common testimony. How much stronger are the evidences of the Christian religion!'

*

The Book of Job explores the nature of God and human suffering. In this extract from a sermon preached on the text: 'In all this Job sinned not, nor charged God foolishly' (Job i.22), Johnson argues for clear and calm consideration of the true nature of God.

Many of the errors of mankind, both in opinion and practice, seem to arise originally from mistaken notions of the divine Being, or at least from want of attention to the nature of those attributes which reason, as well as the holy Scriptures, teaches us to assign to him. A temporary forgetfulness has, for the time, the same effect as real ignorance, but has this advantage, that it is much more easily remedied; since it is much less difficult to recollect our own ideas, than to obtain new ones. This is, I suppose, the state of every man amongst us, who is betrayed by his impatience under afflictions to murmur at Heaven.

He knows, when he reflects calmly, that the world is neither eternal, nor independent; that we neither were produced, nor are preserved, by chance. But that heaven and earth, and the whole system of things, were created by an infinite and perfect Being, who still continues to superintend and govern them. He knows that this great Being is infinitely wise, and infinitely good; so that the end which he proposes must necessarily be the final happiness of those beings that depend upon him, and the means, by which he promotes that end, must undoubtedly be the wisest and the best. All this he is sufficiently convinced of, when he is awakened to recollection; but his conviction is over-borne by the sudden gusts of passion, and his impatience hurries him to wicked exclamations, before he can recall to his mind those reasonings, which, if attended to, would stifle every rebellious thought, and change his distrust and discontent into confidence and tranquillity.

It very nearly concerns every man, since every man is exposed, by the nature of human things, to trouble and calamities, to provide against the days of adversity, by making such ideas familiar to his mind as may defend him against any temptations to the sin of 'charging God foolishly'.

It is frequently observed in common life, that some favourite notion or inclination, long indulged, takes such an entire possession of a man's mind, and so engrosses his faculties, as to mingle thoughts perhaps he is not himself conscious of with almost all his conceptions, and influence his whole behaviour. It will often operate on occasions with which it could scarcely be imagined to have any connection, and will discover itself, however it may lie concealed, either in trifling incidents, or important occurrences, when it is least expected or foreseen. It gives a particular direction to every sentiment and action, and carries a man forward, as by a kind of resistless impulse, or insuperable destiny.

As this unbounded dominion of ideas, long entertained by the fancy, and naturalized to the mind, is a very strong argument against suffering ourselves to dwell too long upon pleasing dreams, or delightful falsehoods, or admitting any inordinate passion to insinuate itself, and grow domestic; so it is a reason, of equal force, to engage us in a frequent, and intense meditation of those important and eternal rules, which are to regulate our conduct, and rectify our minds; that the power of habit may be added to that of truth, that the most useful ideas may be the most familiar, and that every action of our lives may be carried on under the superintendence of an over-ruling piety.

The man who has accustomed himself to consider that he is always in the presence of the Supreme Being, that every work of his hands is carried on, and every imagination of his heart formed, under the inspection of his Creator, and his Judge, easily withstands those temptations which find a ready passage into a mind not guarded and secured by this awful sense of the divine presence.

He is not enticed by ill examples, because the purity of God always occurs to his imagination; he is not betrayed to security by solitude, because he never considers himself as alone.

*

The importance of Scripture to Johnson is shown in the following letter to William Drummond, an Edinburgh bookseller. There was, at the time, a question among Scottish ministers as to whether the New Testament should be translated into Gaelic, which would be expensive. It had the further disadvantage in that there was a desire to make the Highlanders learn English and break down their social and political isolation.

TO MR. WILLIAM DRUMMOND

13th August, 1766

SIR,

I did not expect to hear that it could be, in an assembly convened for the propagation of Christian knowledge, a question whether any nation uninstructed in religion should receive instruction; or whether that instruction should be imparted to them by a translation of the holy books into their own language. If obedience to the will of God be necessary to happiness, and knowledge of his will be necessary to obedience, I know not how he that withholds this knowledge, or delays it, can be said to love his neighbour as himself. He, that voluntarily continues ignorance, is guilty of all the crimes which ignorance produces; as to him that should extinguish the tapers of a light-house, might justly be imputed the calamities of shipwrecks. Christianity is the highest perfection of humanity; and as no man is good but as he wishes the good of others, no man can be good in the highest degree, who wishes not to others the largest measures of the greatest good. To omit for a year, or for a day, the most efficacious method of advancing Christianity, in compliance with any purposes that terminate on this side of the grave, is a crime of which I know not that the world has yet had an example, except in the practice of the planters of America, a race of mortals whom, I suppose, no other man wishes to resemble.

The Papists have, indeed, denied to the laity the use of the bible; but this prohibition, in few places now very rigorously enforced, is defended by arguments which have for their foundation the care of souls. To obscure, upon motives merely political, the light of revelation, is a practice reserved for the reformed; and; surely, the blackest midnight of popery is meridian sunshine to such a reformation. . . .

Elsewhere, Boswell makes this note:

We talked of Kennicott's edition of the Hebrew Bible, and hoped it would be quite faithful. JOHNSON: 'Sir, I know not any crime so great that a man could contrive to commit, as poisoning the sources of eternal truth.'

*

Johnson defends Christopher Smart, the poet, who was confined in a lunatic asylum:

Madness frequently discovers itself merely by unnecessary deviation from the usual modes of the world. My poor friend Smart showed the disturbance of his mind by falling upon his knees and saying his prayers in the street, or in any other unusual place. Now, although, rationally speaking, it is greater madness not to pray at all, than to pray as Smart did, I am afraid there are so many who do not pray, that their understanding is not called in question. . . .

I did not think he ought to be shut up. His infirmities were not noxious to society. He insisted on people praying with him; and I'd as lief pray with Kit Smart as any one else. Another charge was, that he did not love clean linen; and I have no passion for it.

*

Johnson's ironical attack on Soame Jenyns' A Free Inquiry into the Nature and Origin of Evil must gain extra pointedness from the fact that he both saw and felt human suffering to a great degree. Submission to the Creator, as taught by the Bible, was Johnson's only defence against giving way to depression or the kind of folly of Soame Jenyns:

. . . Having thus dispatched the consideration of particular evils, he comes at last to a general reason for which *evil* may be said to be *our good.* He is of opinion that there is some inconceivable benefit in pain abstractedly considered; that pain however inflicted, or wherever felt, communicates some good to the generality of being, and that every animal is some way or other the better for the pain of every other animal. This opinion he carries so far as to suppose that there passes some principle of union through all animal life, as attraction is communicated to all corporeal nature, and that the evils suffered on this globe, may by some inconceivable means contribute to the felicity of the inhabitants of the remotest planet.

How the origin of evil is brought nearer to human conception by any *inconceivable* means, I am not able to discover. We believed that the present system of creation was right, though we could not explain the adaptation of one part to the other, or for the whole succession of causes and consequences. Where has this enquirer added to the little knowledge that we had before? He has told us of the benefits of evil, which no man feels, and relations between distant parts of [the] universe, which he cannot himself conceive. There was enough in this question inconceivable before, and we have little advantage from a new inconceivable solution.

I do not mean to reproach this author for not knowing what is equally hidden from learning and from ignorance. The shame is to impose words for ideas upon ourselves or others. To imagine that we are going forward when we are only turning round. To think that there is any difference between him that gives no reason, and him that gives a reason, which by his own confession cannot be conceived.

But that he may not be thought to conceive nothing but things inconceivable, he has at last thought on a way by which human sufferings may produce good effects. He imagines that as we have not only animals for food, but choose some for our diversion, the same privilege may be allowed to some beings above us, *who may deceive, torment, or destroy us for the ends only of their own pleasure or utility*. This he again finds impossible to be conceived, *but that impossibility lessens not the probability of the conjecture, which by analogy is so strongly confirmed*.

I cannot resist the temptation of contemplating this analogy, which I think he might have carried further very much to the advantage of his argument. He might have shown that these *hunters whose game is man* have many sports analogous to our own. As we drown whelps and kittens, they amuse themselves now and then with sinking a ship, and stand round the fields of *Blenheim* or the walls of *Prague*, as we encircle a cock-pit. As we shoot a bird flying, they take a man in the midst of his business or pleasure, and knock him down with an apoplexy. Some of them, perhaps, are virtuosi, and delight in the operations of an asthma, as a human philosopher in the effects of an air pump. To swell a man with a tympany is as good sport as to blow a frog. Many a merry bout have these frolic beings at the vicissitudes of an ague, and good sport it is to see a man tumble with an epilepsy, and revive and tumble again, and all this he knows not why. As they are wiser and more powerful than we, they have more exquisite diversions, for we have no way of procuring any sport so brisk and so lasting as the paroxysms of the gout and stone which undoubtedly must make high mirth, especially if the play be a little diversified with the blunders and puzzles of the blind and deaf. We know not how far their sphere of observation may extend. Perhaps now and then a merry being may place himself in such a situation as to enjoy at once all the varieties of an epidemical disease, or amuse his leisure with the tossings and contortions of every possible pain exhibited together.

One sport the merry malice of these beings has found means of enjoying to which we have nothing equal or similar. They now and then catch a mortal proud of his parts, and flattered either by the submission of those who court his kindness, or the notice of those who suffer him to court theirs. A head thus prepared for the reception of false opinions, and the projection of vain designs, they easily fill with idle notions, till in time they make their plaything an author: their first diversion commonly begins with an Ode or an epistle, then rises perhaps to a political irony, and is at last brought to its height, by a treatise of philosophy. Then begins the poor animal to entangle himself in sophisms, and flounder in absurdity, to talk confidently of the scale of being, and to give solutions which himself confesses impossible to be understood. Sometimes, however, it happens that their pleasure is without much mischief. The author feels no pain, but while they are wondering at the extravagance of his opinion, and pointing him out to one another as a new example of human folly, he is enjoying his own applause, and that of his companions, and perhaps is elevated with the hope of standing at the head of a new sect.

Many of the books which now crowd the world, may be justly suspected to be written for the sake of some invisible order of beings, for surely they are of no use to any of the corporeal inhabitants of the world. Of the productions of the last bounteous year, how many can be said to serve any purpose of use or pleasure. The only end of writing is to enable the readers better to enjoy life, or better to endure it: and how will either of those be put more in our power by him who tells us, that we are puppets, of which some creature not much wiser than ourselves manages the wires. That a set of beings unseen and unheard, are hovering about us, trying experiments upon our sensibility, putting us in agonies to see our limbs quiver, torturing us to madness, that they may laugh at our vagaries, sometimes obstructing the bile, that they may see how a man looks when he is yellow; sometimes breaking a traveller's bones to try how he will get home; sometimes wasting a man to a skeleton, and sometimes killing him fat for the greater elegance of his hide.

This is an account of natural evil which though, like the rest, not quite new is very entertaining, though I know not how much it may contribute to patience. The only reason why we should contemplate evil is, that we may bear it better, and I am afraid nothing is much more placidly endured, for the sake of making others sport. . . .

CHAPTER 6

His Charity

=====

*Thanks to Boswell, we have many stories about Johnson's charity
– in the best sense of that word. One of the first friends to benefit
from his kindness was Mrs Williams:*

In 1751 we are to consider him as carrying on both his
Dictionary and *Rambler*. Though Johnson's circumstances
were at this time far from being easy, his humane and charitable disposition was constantly exerting itself. Mrs. Anna
Williams, daughter of a very ingenious Welsh physician, and a
woman of more than ordinary talents and literature, having
come to London in hopes of being cured of a cataract in both
her eyes, which afterwards ended in total blindness, was
kindly received as a constant visitor at his house while Mrs.
Johnson lived; and after her death, having come under his
roof in order to have an operation upon her eyes performed
with more comfort to her than in lodgings, she had an apartment from him during the rest of her life, at all times when he
had a house . . .

*

*The following extract is from a sermon Johnson wrote on the text:
'Finally be ye all of one mind, having compassion one of another,
love as brethren, be pitiful, be courteous.' (I Peter iii.8)*

Wherever the eye is turned it sees much misery, and there is
much which it sees not; many complaints are heard, and there
are many pangs without complaint. The external acts of
mercy, to feed the hungry, to clothe the naked, and to visit
the sick, and the prisoners, we see daily opportunities of
performing, and it may be hoped, they are not neglected by
those that abound with what others want.

But there are other calls upon charity. There are sick minds as well as sick bodies; there are understandings perplexed with scruples, there are consciences tormented with guilt; nor can any greater benefit be conferred, than that of settling doubts, or comforting despair, and restoring a disquieted soul to hope and tranquillity.

The duty of commiseration is so strongly pressed by the gospel, that none deny its obligation. But as the measures of beneficence are left undefined, every man necessarily determines for himself, whether he has contributed his share to the necessities of others; and amidst the general depravity of the world, it can be no wonder if there are found some who tax themselves very lightly, and are satisfied with giving very little.

Some readily find out, that where there is distress there is vice, and easily discover the crime of feeding the lazy, or encouraging the dissolute. To promote vice is certainly unlawful, but we do not always encourage vice when we relieve the vicious. It is sufficient that our brother is in want; by which way he brought his want upon him let us not too curiously enquire. We likewise are sinners. In cases undoubted and notorious, some caution may be properly used, that charity be not perverted; but no man is so bad as to lose his title to Christian kindness. If a bad man be suffered to perish, how shall he repent? . . .

That a precept of courtesy is by no means unworthy of the gravity and dignity of an apostolical mandate, may be gathered from the pernicious effects which all must have observed to have arisen from harsh strictness and sour virtue; such as refuses to mingle in harmless gaiety, or give countenance to innocent amusements, or which transacts the petty business of the day with a gloomy ferociousness that clouds existence. Goodness of this character is more formidable than lovely; it may drive away vice from its presence, but will never persuade it to stay and be amended; it may teach, it may remonstrate, but the hearer will seek for more mild instruction. To those, therefore, by whose conversation the heathens were to be drawn away from error and wickedness; it is the

Apostle's precept, that they be courteous, that they accommodate themselves, as far as innocence allows, to the will of others; that they should practise all the established modes of civility, seize all occasions of cultivating kindness, and live with the rest of the world in an amicable reciprocation of cursory civility, that Christianity might not be accused of making men less cheerful as companions, less sociable as neighbours, or less useful as friends.

*

Here is another extract from his sermon on the text: 'Man that is born of woman, is of few days, and full of trouble.' (Job xiv.1)

When we have leisure from our own cares to cast our eyes about us, and behold the whole creation groaning in misery, we must be careful that our judgement is not presumptuous, and that our charity is not regulated by external appearances. We are not to consider those on whom evil falls, as the outcasts of Providence; for though temporal prosperity was promised to the Jews, as a reward of faithful adherence to the worship of God, yet under the dispensation of the gospel we are no where taught, that the good shall have any exemption from the common accidents of life, or that natural and civil evil shall not be equally shared by the righteous and the wicked.

The frequency of misfortunes, and universality of misery may properly repress any tendency to discontent or murmur. We suffer only what is suffered by others, and often by those who are better than ourselves.

But the chief reason why we should send out our enquiries, to collect intelligence of misery, is, that we may find opportunities of doing good. Many human troubles are such as God has given man the power of alleviating. The wants of poverty may evidently be removed by the kindness of those who have more than their own use requires. Of such beneficence the time in which we live does not want examples; and surely that duty can never be neglected, to which so great rewards are so explicitly promised.

But the power of doing good is not confined to the wealthy. He that has nothing else to give, may often give advice. Wisdom likewise has benefits in its power. A wise man may reclaim the vicious, and instruct the ignorant, may quiet the throbs of sorrow, or disentangle the perplexities of conscience. He may compose the resentful, encourage the timorous, and animate the hopeless. In the multifarious afflictions, with which every state of human life is acquainted, there is place for a thousand offices of tenderness; so that he, whose desire it is to do good, can never be long without an opportunity; and every opportunity that Providence presents, let us seize with eagerness, and improve with diligence; remembering that we have no time to lose, for 'man that is born of a woman is of few days.'

*

In 1762, King George III granted Johnson a pension of £300 a year. Mrs Thrale records this in her memoirs:

The addition of three hundred pounds a year, to what Johnson was able to earn by the ordinary exercise of his talents, raised him to a state of comparative affluence, and afforded him the means of assisting many whose real or pretended wants had formerly excited his compassion. He now practised a rule which he often recommended to his friends, always to go abroad with some loose money to give to beggars.

He loved the poor as I never yet saw any one else do, with an earnest desire to make them happy. What signifies, says some one, giving halfpence to common beggars? They only lay it out in gin or tobacco. 'And why (says Johnson) should they be denied such sweeteners of their existence? It is surely very savage to refuse them every possible avenue to pleasure, reckoned too coarse for our own acceptance. Life is a pill which none of us can bear to swallow without gilding; yet for the poor we delight in stripping it still barer, and are not ashamed to show even visible displeasure, if ever the bitter taste is taken from their mouths.' In consequence of these principles he nursed whole nests of people in his house, where the lame, the blind, the sick, and the sorrowful found a sure retreat from all the evils whence his little income could secure them.

Here is just one instance from Boswell:

Coming home late one night, he found a poor woman lying in the street, so much exhausted that she could not walk; he took her upon his back and carried her to his house, where he discovered that she was one of those wretched females who had fallen into the lowest state of vice, poverty and disease. Instead of harshly upbraiding her, he had her taken care of with all tenderness for a long time, at a considerable expense, till she was restored to health, and endeavoured to put her into a virtuous way of living.

Johnson was on occasions driven to take steps to protect himself from his generosity:

When visiting Lichfield, towards the latter part of his life, he was accustomed, on his arrival, to deposit with Miss Porter as much cash as would pay his expenses back to London. He could not trust himself with his own money, as he felt himself unable to resist the importunity of the numerous claimants on his benevolence.

Boswell continues with the praise of his friend:

Johnson's love of little children, which he discovered upon all occasions, calling them 'pretty dears', and giving them sweet-meats, was an undoubted proof of the real humanity and gentleness of his disposition.

His uncommon kindness to his servants, and serious concern, not only for their comfort in this world, but their happiness in the next, was another unquestionable evidence of what all, who were intimately acquainted with him, knew to be true.

Nor would it be just, under this head, to omit the fondness which he showed for animals which he had taken under his protection. I shall never forget the indulgence with which he treated Hodge, his cat; for whom he himself used to go out and buy oysters, lest the servants, having that trouble, should take a dislike to the poor creature . . . I recollect him one day scrambling up Dr Johnson's breast, apparently with much satisfaction, while my friend, smiling and half-whistling, rubbed down his back, and pulled him by the tail; and when I observed he was a fine cat, saying, 'Why, yes, Sir, but I have had cats whom I liked better than this'; and then, as if perceiving Hodge to be out of countenance, adding, 'But he is a very fine cat, a very fine cat indeed.'

'But he is a very fine cat'

Johnson was never a victim of that misapprehension that negroes were an inferior race, which was widespread at that time. The abolition of slavery was not made legal until 1833. Boswell admits this difference between them:

After supper I accompanied him to his apartment, and at my request he dictated to me an argument in favour of the negro who was then claiming his liberty, in an action in the court of session in Scotland. He had always been very zealous against slavery in every form, in which I with all deference thought that he discovered 'a zeal without knowledge' . . .

The Doctor's own trusted personal servant was a negro, and Johnson was more than ordinarily kind to him, twice taking him back into his service after they had parted company.

Johnson was never worried about his own reputation (winning himself the respect of Boswell, who was) and so had no qualms about standing by the disgraced:

Here is a proper place to give an account of Johnson's humane and zealous interference in behalf of the Reverend Dr. William Dodd, formerly prebendary of Brecon, and chaplain in ordinary to his majesty; celebrated as a very popular preacher, an encourager of charitable institutions, and author of a variety of works, chiefly theological. Having unhappily contracted expensive habits of living, partly occasioned by licentiousness of manners, he in an evil hour, when pressed by want of money, and dreading an exposure of his circumstances, forged a bond, of which he attempted to avail himself to support his credit, flattering himself with hopes that he might be able to repay its amount without being detected. The person whose name he thus rashly and criminally presumed to falsify was the Earl of Chesterfield, to whom he had been tutor, and who he perhaps, in the warmth of his feelings, flattered himself would have generously paid the money in case of an alarm being taken, rather than suffer him to fall a victim to the dreadful consequences of violating the law against forgery, the most dangerous crime in a commercial country: but the unfortunate divine had the mortification to find that he was mistaken. His noble pupil appeared against him, and he was capitally convicted.

Johnson made 'extraordinary exertions' on Dodd's behalf, writing many letters and petitions, including one to the king, and a speech for Dodd to deliver at the Old Bailey before the sentence was given, and a sermon to preach before his fellow-prisoners before the execution. Here is his last letter to Dodd:

TO THE REVEREND DR. DODD

June 26, 1777

DEAR SIR,

That which is appointed to all men is now coming upon you. Outward circumstances, the eyes and the thoughts of men, are below the notice of an immortal being about to stand the trial for eternity, before the Supreme Judge of heaven and earth. Be comforted: your crime, morally or religiously considered, has no very deep dye of turpitude. It corrupted no man's principles; it attacked no man's life. It involved only a temporary and reparable injury. Of this, and of all other sins, you are earnestly to repent; and may God, who knoweth our frailty, and desireth not our death, accept your repentance, for the sake of his Son Jesus Christ, our Lord!

In requital of those well-intended offices which you are pleased so emphatically to acknowledge, let me beg that you make in your devotions one petition for my eternal welfare. I am, dear Sir, your most affectionate servant,

SAM. JOHNSON

*

The last extract in this chapter is from a sermon which Johnson composed, perhaps for a service to raise money for a charity school, on the text: 'Every man according as he purposeth in his heart, so let him give; not grudgingly, or of necessity: for God loveth a cheerful giver.' (II Corinthians ix.7)

Every man, who has either applied himself to the examination of his own conduct with care proportioned to the importance of the enquiry, or indulged himself in the more frequent employment of inspecting the behaviour of others, has had many opportunities of observing, with how much difficulty the precepts of religion are long preserved in their full force; how insensibly the ways of virtue are forsaken, and into what depravity those who trust too much to their own strength, sometimes fall, by neglecting to press forward, and to confirm their resolution, by the same methods as they at first excited it. Innumerable temptations continually surround us, and innumerable obstructions oppose us. We are lulled with indolence, we are seduced by pleasure, we are perverted by bad examples, and we are betrayed by our own hearts. No sooner do we, in compliance either with the vanities, or the business, of life, relax our attention to the doctrines of piety, than we grow cold and indifferent, dilatory and negligent. When we are again called to our duty, we find our minds entangled with a thousand objections; we are ready to plead every avocation, however trifling, as an exemption from the necessity of holy practices; and, because we readily satisfy *ourselves* with our excuses, we are willing to imagine that we shall satisfy God, the God of infinite holiness and justice, who sees the most secret motions of our minds, who penetrates through all our hypocrisy, and upon whom disinclination can be never imposed for inability.

With regard to the duty of charity, it is too common for men of avaricious and worldly dispositions, to imagine that they may be saved without compliance with a command so little agreeable to their inclinations; and therefore, though perhaps they cannot always resist the force of argument, or repel conviction at its assault, yet, as they do not willingly suffer their minds to dwell upon reasonings, which they scarcely wish to be true, or renew, by frequent recollection, that sense of their duty which they have received, they quickly relapse into their former sordid insensibility, and, by indulging every consideration which can be applied to the justification of parsimony, harden their hearts, and withhold their hands; and while they see the anguish of misery, and hear the cries of want, can pass by without pity and without regard; and without even feeling any reproaches from their hearts, pray to

God for that mercy, which they have themselves denied to their fellow-beings.

One of the pleas, which is alleged in justification of the neglect of charity, is inability to practise it; an excuse, when real, to which no objection can be made; for it cannot be expected, that any man should give to another what he must himself want in the same degree. But this excuse is too frequently offered by those who are poor only in their own opinion, who have habituated themselves to look on those that are above, rather than on those that are below them, and cannot account themselves rich, while they see any richer; men who measure their revenues, not by the wants of nature, but by the demands of vanity; and who have nothing to give, only because they will not diminish any particle of their splendour, nor reduce the pomp of their equipage; who, while their tables are heaped with delicacies, and their houses crowded with festal assemblies, suffer the poor to languish in the streets in miseries and in want, complain that their fortunes are not equal to the generosity of their minds, and applaud their own inclinations to charity and mercy: inclinations which are never exerted in beneficence, because they cannot spare any thing from their appetites and their pride.

Others there are, who frequently delight to dwell upon the excellency of charity, and profess themselves ready to comply with its precepts, whenever proper objects shall be proposed, and an opportunity of proper application shall be found; but they pretend that they are so *well* informed, with regard to the perversion of charity, and discover so many ill effects of indistinguishing and careless liberality, that they are not easily satisfied with the occasions which are offered them. They are sometimes afraid of encouraging idleness, and sometimes of countenancing imposture, and so readily find objections to every method of charity that can be mentioned to them, that their good inclinations are of very little advantage to the rest of mankind; but however they congratulate themselves upon their merit, and still applaud that generosity by which calamity was never softened, and by which want never was relieved.

CHAPTER 7

His Christian Life

━━━

*To follow anyone, and most of all, to follow Jesus, one's greatest
need is for watchfulness. Johnson's attack is on all classes of men
and women, those 'peaceable and temperate heathens' who are
spiritually fast asleep or deluding themselves. If the Gospel is true,
then it demands a response, but as Johnson says:*

Of self-deceit, in the great business of our lives, there are
various modes. The far greater part of mankind deceive themselves by willing negligence, by refusing to think on their real
state, lest such thoughts should trouble their quiet, or inter-
rupt their pursuits. To live religiously, is to walk, not by sight,
but by faith; to act in confidence of things unseen, in hope of
future recompence, and in fear of future punishment. To
abstract the thoughts from things spiritual is not difficult;
things future do not obtrude themselves upon the senses, and
therefore easily give way to external objects. He that is willing
to forget religion, may quickly lose it; and that most men are
willing to forget it, experience informs us. If we look into the
gay, or the busy world, we see every eye directed towards
pleasure or advantage, and every hour filled with expectation,
or occupied by employment, and day passed after day in the
enjoyment of success, or the vexation of disappointment.

Nor is it true only of men, who are engaged in enterprises of
hazard, which restrain the faculties to the utmost, and keep
attention always upon the stretch. Religion is not only neglected by the projector and adventurer, by men, who suspend
their happiness on the slender thread of artifice, or stand
tottering upon the point of chance. For if we visit the most
cool and regular parts of the community, if we turn our eye to
the farm, or to the shop, where one year glides uniformly after
another, and nothing new or important is either expected or

dreaded; yet still the same indifference about eternity will be found. There is no interest so small, nor engagement so slight, but that if it be followed and expanded, it may be sufficient to keep religion out of the thoughts. Many men may be observed, not agitated by very violent passions, nor overborne by any powerful habits, nor depraved by any great degrees of wickedness; men who are honest dealers, faithful friends, and inoffensive neighbours; who yet have no vital principle of religion; who live wholly without self-examination; and indulge any desire that happens to arise, with very little resistance, or compunction; who hardly know, what it is to combat a temptation, or to repent of a fault; but go on, neither self-approved, nor self-condemned; not endeavouring after any excellence, nor reforming any vicious practice, or irregular desire. They have no care of futurity, neither is God in all their thoughts; they direct none of their actions to his glory, they do nothing with the hope of pleasing, they avoid nothing for fear of offending him. Those men want not much of being religious, they have nothing more than casual views to reform, and from being peaceable and temperate heathens, might, if they would once awaken to their eternal interest, become pious and exemplary Christians. But let them not be deceived, they cannot suppose that God will accept him, who never wished to be accepted by him, or made his will the rule of action.

Others there are, who, without attending to the written revelation of God's will, form to themselves a scheme of conduct, in which vice is mingled with virtue, and who cover from themselves, and hope to cover from God, the indulgence of some criminal desire, or the continuance of some vicious habit, by a few splendid instances of public spirit, or some few effusions of occasional bounty. But to these men it may, with emphatical propriety, be urged, that God is not mocked; he will not be worshipped nor obeyed, but according to his own laws. *(From a sermon on the text: 'Be not deceived, God is not mocked; for whatsoever a man soweth, that shall he reap.' Galatians vi.7)*

*

62

In the next sermon, Johnson speaks from his own experience about broken resolutions. He also brilliantly exposes our weakness for cherishing our own virtues, but ignoring our faults.

To give the heart to God, and to give the whole heart, is very difficult; the last, the great effort of long labour, fervent prayer, and diligent meditation. – Many resolutions are made, and many relapses lamented, and many conflicts with our own desires, with the powers of this world, and the powers of darkness, must be sustained, before the will of man is made wholly obedient to the will of God.

In the mean time, we are willing to find some way to heaven, less difficult and less obstructed, to keep our hopes alive by faint endeavours, and to lull our consciences by such expedients, as we may easily practise. Not yet resolved to live wholly to God, and yet afraid to live wholly to the world, we do something in recompence for that which we neglect, and resign something that we may keep the rest.

To be strictly religious is difficult; but we may be zealously religious at little expence. – By expressing on all occasions our detestation of heresy and popery, and all other errors, we erect ourselves into champions for truth, without much hazard or trouble. – The hopes of zeal are not wholly groundless. – Indifference in questions of importance is no amiable quality. – He that is warm for truth, and fearless in its defence, performs one of the duties of a good man; he strengthens his own conviction, and guards others from delusion; but steadiness of belief, and boldness of profession, are yet only part of the form of godliness, which may be attained by those who deny the power.

As almost every man is, by nature or by accident, exposed to danger from particular temptations, and disposed to some vices more than to others; so all are, either by disposition of mind, or the circumstances of life, inclined or impelled to some laudable practices. Of this happy tendency it is common to take advantage, by pushing the favourite, or the convenient, virtue to its utmost extent, and to lose all sense of deficiency in the perpetual contemplation of some single excellence.

Thus some please themselves with a constant regularity of life, and decency of behaviour, – they hear themselves commended, and superadd their own approbation. They know, or might know, that they have secret faults; but, as they are not open to accusation, they are not inquisitive to their own disquiet; they are satisfied that they do not corrupt others, and that the world will not be worse by their example.

Some are punctual in the attendance on public worship, and perhaps in the performance of private devotion. These they know to be great duties, and resolve not to neglect them. It is right they go so far; and with so much that is right they are satisfied. They are diligent in adoration, but defective in obedience.

Such men are often not hypocrites; the virtues which they practise arise from their principles. The man of regularity really hopes, that he shall recommend goodness to those that know him. The frequenter of the church really hopes to propitiate his Creator. Their religion is sincere; what is reprehensible is, that it is partial, that the heart is yet not purified, and that yet many inordinate desires remain, not only unsubdued, but unsuspected, under the splendid cover of some specious practice, with which the mind delights itself too much, to take a rigorous survey of its own motions.

In condemnation of those who presume to hope, that the performance of one duty will obtain excuse for the violation of others, it is affirmed by St. James, that he who breaks one commandment is guilty of all; and he defends his position by observing, that they are all delivered by the same authority.

His meaning is not, that all crimes are equal, or that in any one crime all others are involved, but that the law of God is to be obeyed with complete and unreserved submission; and that he who violates any of its ordinances, will not be justified by his observation of all the rest, since as the whole is of divine authority, every breach, wilful and unrepented, is an act of rebellion against Omnipotence.

One of the artifices, by which men, thus defectively religious, deceive themselves, is that of comparing their own behaviour with that of men openly vicious, and generally negligent; and inferring that themselves are good, because they suppose that they see others worse. The account of the Pharisee and Publican may show us that, in rating our own merit, we are in danger of mistake. But though the estimate should be right, it is still to be remembered, that he who is not worst, may yet fall far below what will be required. Our rule of duty is not *the virtue of men*, but *the law of God*, from which alone we can learn what will be required . . . *(From a sermon on the text: 'Having a form of godliness, but denying the power thereof.' II Timothy iii.5)*

*

One of Dr Johnson's most frequent resolutions was to read the Bible methodically. He would have known it very thoroughly, but in his anxiety to understand and please God, he was rarely satisfied with his knowledge. It is salutary to read this note which he made in 1772:

APR 26. . . . It is a comfort to me that, at last, in my sixty third year, I have attained to know, even thus hastily, confusedly, and imperfectly, what my Bible contains.

May the good God increase and sanctify my knowledge.

*

The following conversation recorded by Boswell is interesting, and not only because it was one of the few in which Johnson was worsted:

Dr. Mayo having asked Johnson's opinion of Soame Jenyns's 'View of the Internal Evidence of the Christian Religion,' – JOHNSON: 'I think it a pretty book; not very theological, indeed; and there seems to be an affectation of ease and carelessness, as if it were not suitable to his character to be very serious about the matter.' BOSWELL: '*You* should like his book, Mrs. Knowles, as it maintains, as you *friends* do, that courage is not a Christian virtue.' MRS. KNOWLES: 'Yes, indeed, I like him there; but I cannot agree with him that friendship is not a Christian virtue.' JOHNSON: 'Why, Madam, strictly speaking, he is right. All friendship is preferring the interest of a friend to the neglect, or, perhaps, against the interest, of others; so that an old Greek said, "He that has *friends* has no *friend*." Now, Christianity recommends universal benevolence; to consider all men as our brethren; which is contrary to the virtue of friendship, as described by the ancient philosophers. Surely, Madam, your sect must approve of this; for you call all men *friends*.' MRS. KNOWLES: 'We are commanded to do good to all men, "but especially to them who are of the household of faith." ' JOHNSON: 'Well, Madam; the household of faith is wide enough.' MRS. KNOWLES: 'But, Doctor, our Saviour had twelve apostles, yet there was *one* whom he *loved*. John was called "the disciple whom Jesus loved." ' JOHNSON (with eyes sparkling benignantly): 'Very well indeed, Madam. You have said very well.' BOSWELL: 'A fine application. Pray, Sir, had you ever thought of it?' JOHNSON: 'I had not, Sir.'

*

One of Johnson's greatest (and most unlikely) friends was the 'huntin', shootin', fishin' ' rector of Ashbourne, John Taylor, for whom he wrote most of his sermons. Perhaps this response to a light-hearted comment was made with Taylor in mind:

'Sir, the life of a parson, of a conscientious clergyman, is not easy. I have always considered a clergyman as the father of a larger family than he is able to maintain. I would rather have Chancery suits upon my hands than the cure of souls. No, Sir, I do not envy a clergyman's life as an easy life, nor do I envy the clergyman who makes it an easy life.'

He also took very seriously the proper observance of Sundays.

'It should be different from another day. People may walk, but not throw stones at birds. There may be relaxation, but there should be no levity.'

*

Observance of Easter was particularly important to Johnson, as he made his Communion then, and preceded this by rigorous self-examination. At that time such an infrequent Communion was common, the idea being that much preparation was required before the Christian was worthy to partake of it. Johnson wrote this meditation in 1771.

A meditation on RECEIVING THE SACRAMENT

I profess my Faith in Jesus. I declare my resolution to obey him. I implore in the highest act of worship Grace to keep these resolutions.

I hope to rise to a new life this day.

I did not this week labour my preparation so much as I have sometimes done. My Mind was not very quiet; and an anxious preparation makes the duty of the day formidable and burdensome. Different methods suit different states of mind, body, and affairs. I rose this day, and prayed, then went to tea, and afterwards composed the prayer, which I formed with great fluency. I went to church, came in at the Psalms, could not hear the reader in the lessons, but attended the prayers with tranquillity . . .

Here are Boswell and Johnson's parallel accounts of Good Friday, 1773:

On the 9th of April, being Good Friday, I breakfasted with him on tea and cross-buns . . . He carried me with him to the church of St. Clement Danes, where he had his seat; and his behaviour was, as I had imaged to myself, solemnly devout. I never shall forget the tremulous earnestness with which he pronounced the awful petition in the Litany: 'In the hour of death, and at the day of judgment, good Lord deliver us.'

We went to church both in the morning and evening. In the interval between the two services we did not dine; but he read in the Greek New Testament, and I turned over several of his books.

GOOD FRIDAY, APR. 9, 1773. On this day I went twice to Church and Boswell was with me. I had forborn to attend Divine service for some time in the winter, having a cough which would have interrupted both my own attention and that of others, and when the cough grew less troublesome I did

'I did not regain the habit of going to church.'
Boswell and Johnson in the Strand

not regain the habit of going to church, though I did not wholly omit it. I found the service not burthensome nor tedious, though I could not hear the lessons. I hope in time to take pleasure in public Worship.

On this whole day I took nothing of nourishment but one cup of tea without milk, but the fast was very inconvenient. Towards night I grew fretful, and impatient, unable to fix my mind or govern my thoughts, and felt a very uneasy sensation both in my stomach and head, compounded as it seemed of laxity and pain.

From this uneasiness, of which when I was not asleep, I was sensible all night, I was relieved in the morning by drinking tea, and eating the soft part of a penny loaf.

This I have set down for future observation.

Boswell writes again in 1775:

On Friday, April 14, being Good Friday, I repaired to him in the morning, according to my usual custom on that day, and breakfasted with him. I observed that he fasted very strictly, that he did not even taste bread, and took no milk with his tea; I suppose because it is a kind of animal food. . . . In his private register this evening is thus marked, 'Boswell sat with me till night; we had some serious talk.' It also appears from the same record, that after I left him he was occupied in religious duties, in 'giving Francis, his servant, some directions for preparation to communicate; in reviewing his life, and resolving on better conduct.' The humility and piety which he discovers on such occasions is truly edifying. No saint, however, in the course of his religious warfare, was more sensible of the unhappy failure of pious resolves than Johnson. He said one day, talking to an acquaintance on the subject, 'Sir, hell is paved with good intentions.'

*

In 1783, the year before his death, Johnson suffered 'a dreadful stroke of the palsy' (Boswell). He met this new affliction with resignation and fortitude (note his method of testing whether 'the integrity' of his faculties had been affected):

TO MR. EDMUND ALLEN

June 17, 1783

It has pleased God this morning to deprive me of the powers of speech; and as I do not know but that it may be his further good pleasure to deprive me soon of my senses, I request you will, on the receipt of this note, come to me, and act for me as the exigencies of my case may require. I am, &c.,

SAM. JOHNSON

Two days later he wrote to Mrs Thrale:

On Monday, the 16th, I sat for my picture and walked a considerable way with little inconvenience. In the afternoon and evening I felt myself light and easy, and began to plan schemes of life. Thus I went to bed, and in a short time waked and sat up, as has been long my custom, when I felt a confusion and indistinctness in my head, which lasted, I suppose, about half a minute. I was alarmed, and prayed God, that however he might afflict my body, he would spare my understanding. This prayer, that I might try the integrity of my faculties, I made in Latin verse. The lines were not very good, but I knew them not to be very good: I made them easily, and concluded myself to be unimpaired in my faculties . . .

*

In the final year of his life, Johnson seemed to have become less fearful and more trusting in the love of God, whom he had served so long. Boswell recounts an incident, which he feels may have been more than a self-induced sensation:

One morning afterwards, when I found him alone, he communicated to me, with solemn earnestness, the very remarkable circumstance which had happened in the course of his illness, when he was much distressed by the dropsy. He had shut himself up, and employed a day in particular exercises of religion, fasting, humiliation, and prayer. On a sudden he obtained extraordinary relief, for which he looked up to Heaven with grateful devotion. He made no direct inference from this fact; but from his manner of telling it, I could perceive that it appeared to him as something more than an incident in the common course of events. For my own part, I have no difficulty to avow that cast of thinking, which, by many modern pretenders to wisdom, is called *superstitious*. But here I think even men of dry rationality may believe, that there was an intermediate interposition of Divine Providence, and that the 'fervent prayer of this righteous man' availed.

CHAPTER 8

On Churches

———

Johnson's reputation for intolerance and fixed opinions has persisted to this day, but certainly in matters of religion he could be unusually generous, especially to Roman Catholics. Boswell acknowledges this generosity (at a time when Catholics were discriminated against in society) in his account of their first dinner together at the Mitre tavern.

I acknowledged, that though educated very strictly in the principles of religion, I had for some time been misled into a certain degree of infidelity; but that I was come now to a better way of thinking, and was fully satisfied of the truth of the Christian revelation, though I was not clear as to every point considered to be orthodox. Being at all times a curious examiner of the human mind, and pleased with an undisguised display of what had passed in it, he called to me with warmth, 'Give me your hand; I have taken a liking to you.'

After having given credit to reports of his bigotry, I was agreeably surprised when he expressed the following very liberal sentiment: 'For my part, Sir, I think all Christians, whether Papists or Protestants, agree in the essential articles, and that their differences are trivial, and rather political than religious.'

*

Dr Johnson and Boswell visited the ruins of St Andrew's Cathedral on their tour of Scotland and Boswell made the following note:

He kept his hat off while he was upon any part of the ground where the cathedral had stood. He said well, that 'Knox had set on a mob, without knowing where it would end; and that differing from a man in doctrine was no reason why you should pull his house about his ears.' As we walked in the cloisters, there was a solemn echo, while he talked loudly of a proper retirement from the world. 'In general, as every man is obliged not only to "love God, but his neighbour as himself," he must bear his part in active life, yet there are exceptions. Those who are exceedingly scrupulous (which I do not approve, for I am no friend to scruples), and find their scrupulosity invincible, so that they are quite in the dark, and know not what they shall do, – or those who cannot resist temptations, and find they make themselves worse by being in the world, without making it better, – may retire. I never read of a hermit, but in imagination I kiss his feet: never of a monastery, but I could fall on my knees, and kiss the pavement. But I think putting young people there, who know nothing of life, nothing of retirement, is dangerous and wicked. It is a saying as old as Hesiod –

> Let youth in deeds, in counsel man engage:
> Prayer is the proper duty of old age.

That is a very noble line: not that young men should not pray, or old men not give counsel, but that every season of life has its proper duties. I have thought of retiring, and have talked of it to a friend; but I find my vocation is rather to active life.'

*

Johnson was a staunch member of the Church of England (although attending its services was always an effort for him) but he respected Christians of other persuasions. In his Life of Milton *the Doctor made the following observation:*

To be of no church is dangerous. Religion, of which the rewards are distant and which is animated only by Faith and Hope, will glide by degrees out of the mind unless it be invigorated and reimpressed by external ordinances, by stated calls to worship, and the salutary influence of example. Milton, who appears to have had full conviction of the truth of Christianity, and to have regarded the Holy Scriptures with the profoundest veneration, to have been untainted by any

'To be of no church is dangerous.'
Johnson bows to the Archbishop

heretical peculiarity of opinion, and to have lived in a confirmed belief of the immediate and occasional agency of Providence, yet grew old without any visible worship. In the
distribution of his hours, there was no hour of prayer, either
solitary or with his household; omitting public prayers, he
omitted all.

Of this omission the reason has been sought, upon a supposition which ought never to be made, that men live with their approbation, and justify their conduct to themselves. Prayer certainly was not thought superfluous by him, who represents our first parents as praying acceptably in the state of innocence, and efficaciously after their fall. That he lived without prayer can hardly be affirmed; his studies and meditations were an habitual prayer. The neglect of it in his family was probably a fault for which he condemned himself, and which he intended to correct, but that death, as too often happens, intercepted his reformation.

This last paragraph could be written about himself. Johnson was quick to point out that the disparity between a man's beliefs and actions may not necessarily spring from hypocrisy, but may be simply a matter of weakness. In this he speaks, again, from his own painful experience.

In the following sermon, Johnson balances his condemnation of corruption in other churches by a stern warning to his own congregation not to rest complacent about their own.

The professors of Christianity have few ceremonies indispensably enjoined them. Their religion teaches them to worship God, not with local or temporary ceremonies, but in spirit and in truth; that is, with internal purity, and moral righteousness. For spirit, in this sense, seems to be opposed to the body of external rites, and truth is known to signify, in the biblical language, the sum of those duties which we owe to one another.

Yet such are the temptations of interest and pleasure, and so prevalent is the desire of enjoying at once, the pleasures of sin for a season, and the hopes of happiness to eternity; that even the Christian religion has been depraved by artificial modes of piety, and succedaneous practices of reconciliation. Men have been ever persuaded, that by doing something, to which they think themselves not obliged, they may purchase an exemption from such duties as they find themselves inclined to violate: that they may commute with heaven for a temporal fine, and make rigour atone for relaxity.

In ages and countries, in which ignorance has produced, and nourished, superstition; many artifices have been invented, of practising piety without virtue, and repentance without amendment. The devotion of our blind fore-fathers consisted, for a great part, in rigorous austerities, laborious pilgrimages, and gloomy retirement; and that which now prevails, in the darker provinces of the popish world, exhausts its power in absurd veneration for some particular saint, expressed too often by honours paid to his image, or in a stated number of prayers, uttered with very little attention, and very frequently with little understanding.

Some of these practices may be perhaps justly imputed to the grossness of a people, scarcely capable of complying with the weakness of men, who must be taught their duty by material images, and sensible impressions. This plea, however, will avail but little, in defence of abuses not only permitted, but encouraged by pertinaceous vindications, and fictitious miracles.

It is apparent that the Romish clergy have attributed too much efficacy to pious donations, and charitable establishments; and that they have made liberality to the church, and bounty to the poor, equivalent to the whole system of our duty to God, and to our neighbour.

Yet nothing can be more repugnant to the general tenor of the evangelical revelation, than an opinion that pardon may be bought, and guilt effaced, by a stipulated expiation. We naturally catch the pleasures of the present hour, and gratify the calls of the reigning passion: and what shall hinder the man of violence from outrage and mischief, or restrain the pursuer of interest from fraud and circumvention, when they are told, that after a life passed in disturbing the peace of life, and violating the security of possession, they may die at last in peace, by founding an alms-house, without the agonies of deep contrition?

But error and corruption are often to be found where there are neither Jews nor Papists. – Let us not look upon the depravity of others with triumph, nor censure it with bitterness. – Every sect may find, in its own followers, those who have the form of godliness, without the power; every man, if he examines his own conduct, without intention to be his own flatterer, may, to a certain degree, find it in himself. *(From a sermon on the text: 'Having a form of godliness, but denying the power thereof.' II Timothy iii.5)*

*

Pilgrimage, of course, was one of the many practices which the Protestant churches decreed to be unnecessary and superstitious. To the ever-practical Englishman, they have always seemed a waste of time and money, an irresponsible jaunt or pious fantasy. But Johnson was clearly interested in the idea – although he (thinly disguised as Imlac in Rasselas*) pronounces it to be without any supernatural power.*

'Pilgrimage,' said Imlac, 'like many other acts of piety, may be reasonable or superstitious, according to the principles upon which it is performed. Long journeys in search of truth are not commanded. Truth, such as is necessary to the regulation of life, is always found where it is honestly sought. Change of place is no natural cause of the increase of piety, for it inevitably produces dissipation of mind. Yet, since men go every day to view the fields where great actions have been performed, and return with stronger impressions of the event, curiosity of the same kind may naturally dispose us to view that country whence our religion had its beginning; and I believe no man surveys those awful scenes without some confirmation of holy resolutions. That the Supreme Being may be more easily propitiated in one place than in another, is the dream of idle superstition; but that some places may operate upon our own minds in an uncommon manner, is an opinion which hourly experience will justify. He who supposes that his vices may be more successfully combated in Palestine, will, perhaps, find himself mistaken, yet he may go thither without folly; he who thinks they will be more freely pardoned, dishonours at once his reason and religion.'

*

*He writes to Boswell in much the same vein later on in answer to
a letter in which Boswell mentions 'a peculiar satisfaction which
I experienced in celebrating the festival of Easter in St Paul's
Cathedral; that, to my fancy, it appeared like going up to Jerusalem
at the Feast of the Passover; and that the strong devotion which I felt
on that occasion diffused its influence on my mind through the rest
of the year.' One suspects – and perhaps Johnson did too, though he
treats the question seriously – that the Easter in London was not so
much on account of St Paul's Cathedral, but more because of other
attractions afforded by the capital. Boswell adored London almost
as much as his friend, and was always thinking of excuses to make a
visit there after his marriage and succession to his father's estates.*

TO JAMES BOSWELL, ESQ.

[Not dated, but written about 15 March 1774]

DEAR SIR,

. . . Your last reason is so serious, that I am unwilling to
oppose it. Yet you must remember, that your image of wor-
shipping once a year in a certain place, in imitation of the
Jews, is but a comparison; and *simile non est idem:* if the
annual resort to Jerusalem was a duty to the Jews, it was a
duty because it was commanded; and you have no such
command, therefore no such duty. It may be dangerous to
receive too readily, and indulge too fondly, opinions, from
which, perhaps, no pious mind is wholly disengaged, of local
sanctity and local devotion. You know what strange effects
they have produced over a great part of the Christian world. I
am now writing, and you, when you read this, are reading
under the eye of Omnipresence.

To what degree fancy is to be admitted into religious
offices, it would require much deliberation to determine. I am
far from intending totally to exclude it. Fancy is a faculty
bestowed by our Creator, and it is reasonable that all his gifts
should be used to his glory, that all our faculties should co-
operate in his worship; but they are to co-operate according to
the will of him that gave them, according to the order which
his wisdom has established. As ceremonies prudential or
convenient are less obligatory than positive ordinances, as

bodily worship is only the token to others or ourselves of mental adoration, so fancy is always to act in subordination to reason. We may take fancy for a companion, but must follow reason as our guide. We may allow fancy to suggest certain ideas in certain places; but reason must always be heard, when she tells us that those ideas and those places have no natural or necessary relation. When we enter a church we habitually call to mind the duty of adoration, but we must not omit adoration for want of a temple; because we know, and ought to remember, that the Universal Lord is everywhere present; and that, therefore, to come to Iona, or to Jerusalem, though it may be useful, cannot be necessary . . .

*

We see in Boswell the typical attitudes towards Roman Catholics which most British people have held since the Reformation. Johnson did not share them, perhaps because he saw in the Roman Church the certainty of salvation which he craved. The following conversations were recorded by Boswell.

Mrs. Kennicott spoke of her brother, the Reverend Mr. Chamberlayne, who had given up great prospects in the Church of England on his conversion to the Roman Catholic faith. Johnson, who warmly admired every man who acted from a conscientious regard to principle, erroneous or not, exclaimed fervently, 'God bless him.'

On the Roman Catholic religion he said, 'If you join the papists externally, they will not interrogate you strictly as to your belief in their tenets. No reasoning papist believes every article of their faith. There is one side on which a good man might be persuaded to embrace it. A good man of a timorous disposition, in great doubt of his acceptance with God, and pretty credulous, may be glad to be of a church where there are so many helps to get to heaven. I would be a papist if I could. I have fear enough; but an obstinate rationality prevents me. I shall never be a papist, unless on the near approach of death, of which I have a very great terror. I wonder that women are not all papists.' BOSWELL: 'They are not more afraid of death than men are.' JOHNSON: 'Because they are less wicked.' DR. ADAMS: 'They are more pious.' JOHNSON: 'No, hang 'em, they are not more pious. A wicked fellow is the most pious when he takes to it. He'll beat you all at piety.'

I had hired a Bohemian as my servant while I remained in London; and being much pleased with him, I asked Dr. Johnson whether his being a Roman Catholic should prevent my taking him with me to Scotland. JOHNSON: 'Why, no , Sir. If *he* has no objection, you can have none.' BOSWELL: 'So, Sir, you are no great enemy to the Roman Catholic religion.' JOHNSON: 'No more, Sir, than to the Presbyterian religion.' BOSWELL: 'You are joking.' JOHNSON: 'No, Sir, I really think so. Nay, Sir, of the two, I prefer the Popish.' BOSWELL: 'How so, Sir?' JOHNSON: 'Why, Sir, as it was an apostolical institution, I think it is dangerous to be without it. And, Sir, the Presbyterians have no public worship; they have no form of prayer in which they know they are to join. They go to hear a man pray, and are to judge whether they will join with him.' BOSWELL: 'But, Sir, their doctrine is the same with that of the Church of England. Their confession of faith, and the thirty-nine articles, contain the same points, even the doctrine of predestination.' JOHNSON: 'Why, yes, Sir; predestination was a part of the clamour of the times, so it is mentioned in our articles, but with as little positiveness as could be.' BOSWELL: 'Is it necessary, Sir, to believe all the thirty-nine articles?' JOHNSON: 'Why, Sir, that is a question which has been much agitated. Some have thought it necessary that they should all be believed; others have considered them to be only articles of peace, that is to say, you are not to preach against them.' BOSWELL: 'It appears to me, Sir, that predestination, or what is equivalent to it, cannot be avoided, if we hold an universal prescience in the Deity.' JOHNSON: 'Why, Sir, does not God every day see things going on without preventing them?' BOSWELL: 'True, Sir; but if a thing be *certainly* foreseen, it must be fixed, and cannot happen otherwise; and if we apply this consideration to the human mind, there is no free will, nor do I see how prayer can be of any avail.' I did not press it further, when I perceived that he was displeased, and shrunk from any abridgement of an attribute usually ascribed to the Divinity, however irreconcilable in its full extent with the grand system of moral government.

I proceeded: 'What do you think, Sir, of Purgatory, as believed by the Roman Catholics?' JOHNSON: 'Why, Sir, it is a very harmless doctrine. They are of opinion that the generality of mankind are neither so obstinately wicked as to deserve everlasting punishment, nor so good as to merit being admitted into the society of blessed spirits; and therefore that God is graciously pleased to allow of a middle state, where they may be purified by certain degrees of suffering. You see, Sir, there is nothing unreasonable in this.' BOSWELL: 'But then, Sir, their masses for the dead?' JOHNSON: 'Why, Sir, if it be once established that there are souls in purgatory, it is as proper to pray for *them*, as for our brethren of mankind who are yet in this life.' BOSWELL: 'The idolatry of the mass?' – JOHNSON: 'Sir, there is no idolatry in the mass. They believe God to be there, and they adore him.' BOSWELL: 'The worship of saints?' JOHNSON: 'Sir, they do not worship saints; they invoke them; they only ask their prayers. I am talking all this time of the *doctrines* of the Church of Rome. I grant you that, in *practice*, purgatory is made a lucrative imposition, and that the people do become idolatrous as they recommend themselves to the tutelary protection of particular saints. I think their giving the sacrament only in one kind is criminal, because it is contrary to the express institution of Christ, and I wonder how the Council of Trent admitted it.' BOSWELL: 'Confession?' JOHNSON: 'Why, I don't know but that is a good thing. The Scripture says, "Confess your faults one to another," and the priests confess as well as the laity. Then it must be considered that their absolution is only upon repentance, and often upon penance also. You think your sins may be forgiven without penance, upon repentance alone.'

I thus ventured to mention all the common objections against the Roman Catholic church, that I might hear so great a man upon them. What he said is here accurately recorded.

But it is not improbable that, if one had taken the other side, he might have reasoned differently.

I must however mention, that he had a respect for 'the old religion' as the mild Melanchthon called that of the Roman Catholic church, even while he was exerting himself for its reformation in some particulars. Sir William Scott informs me, that he heard Johnson say, 'A man who is converted from Protestantism to Popery, may be sincere; he parts with nothing: he is only superadding to what he already had. But a convert from Popery to Protestantism gives up so much of what he has held as sacred as any thing that he retains – there is so much *laceration of mind* in such a conversion – that it can hardly be sincere and lasting.'

*

Johnson was not, however, so sympathetic about the new young upstart, Methodism. He would have distrusted any movement which placed such an emphasis on personal religious feelings rather than rational argument and which broke away from the objective authority of an episcopal church. Boswell gives us the following notes of Johnson's distinct lack of enthusiasm for those people commonly called 'enthusiasts'.

Speaking of the *inward light*, to which some Methodists pretended, he said, it was a principle utterly incompatible with social or civil security. 'If a man,' said he, 'pretends to a principle of action of which I can know nothing, nay, not so much as that he has it, but only that he pretends to it; how can I tell what that person may be prompted to do? When a person professes to be governed by a written ascertained law, I can then know where to find him.'

Two young women from Staffordshire visited him when I was present, to consult him on the subject of Methodism, to which they were inclined. 'Come,' said he, 'you pretty fools, dine with Maxwell and me at the Mitre, and we will talk over that subject', which they did, and after dinner he took one of them upon his knee, and fondled her for half an hour together.

*

In Johnson's diaries for 1765 we find the following note:

I invited home with me the man whose pious behaviour I had for several years observed on this day, and found him a kind of Methodist, full of texts, but ill-instructed. I talked to him with temper, and offered him wine which he refused. I suffered him to go without the dinner which I had purposed to give him. I thought this day that there was something irregular and particular in his look and gesture, but having intended to invite him to acquaintance, and having a fair opportunity by finding him near my own seat after I had missed him, I did what I at first designed, and am sorry to have been so much disappointed. Let me not be prejudiced hereafter against the appearance of piety in mean persons, who, with indeterminate notions, and perverse or inelegant conversation perhaps are doing all that they can.

CHAPTER 9

On Repentance

===

Johnson's habitual attitude of penitence was the logical outcome of his beliefs; if the Gospel is true then the best of us are no more than 'unprofitable servants'.

SUNDAY, JULY 13, 1755. Having lived hitherto in perpetual neglect of public worship & though for some years past not without an habitual reverence for the sabbath yet without that attention to its religious duties which Christianity requires I will once more form a scheme of life for that day such as alas I have often vainly formed which when my mind is capable of settled practice I hope to follow.

1 To rise early and in order to [do] it to go to sleep early on saturday.
2 To use some extraordinary devotion in the morning.
3 To examine the tenor of my life & particularly the last week & to mark my advances in religion or recession from it.
4 To read the Scripture methodically with such helps as are at hand.
5 To go to church twice.
6 To read books of divinity either speculative or practical.
7 To instruct my family.
8 To wear off by meditation any worldly soil contracted in the week.

*

It was Johnson's custom to examine his conscience three times a year, at Easter, on his birthday, and on New Year's Day. The turning of the year was an emotional time for a man so dogged by thoughts of mortality. Here is his prayer for New Year's Day 1745.

Almighty and everlasting God, in whose hands are life and death, by whose will all things were created, and by whose providence they are sustained, I return thee thanks that thou hast given me life, and that thou hast continued it to this time, that thou hast hitherto forborn to snatch me away in the midst of Sin and Folly, and hast permitted me still to enjoy the means of Grace, and vouchsafed to call me yet again to Repentance. Grant, O merciful Lord, that thy Call may not be in vain, that my Life may not be continued to increase my Guilt, and that thy gracious Forbearance may not harden my heart in wickedness. Let me remember, O my God, that as Days and Years pass over me, I approach nearer to the Grave, where there is no repentance, and grant, that by the assistance of thy Holy Spirit, I may so pass through this Life, that I may obtain Life everlasting, for the Sake of our Lord Jesus Christ. Amen.

*

Johnson observed Good Friday strictly and liked to fast, although he found it very difficult. (Dr Samuel Clarke [1675–1729] was unorthodox in some of his views on the Trinity but Johnson admired his sermons.)

GOOD FRIDAY, MARCH 28, 1766. On the night before I used proper collects, and prayed when I awoke in the morning. I had all the week an awe upon me, not thinking on passion week till I looked in the almanack. I have wholly forborn M[eat] and wine except one glass on Sunday night.

In the morning I rose, and drank very small tea without milk, and had nothing more that day.

This was the day on which Tetty died. I did not mingle much men[tion] of her with the devotions of this day, because it is dedicated to more holy subjects. I mentioned her at church and prayed once solemnly at home.

I was twice at church, and went through the prayers without perturbation. But heard the sermons imperfectly. I came in both times at the second lesson, not hearing the bell.

When I came home I read the psalms for the day, and one

sermon in Clarke. Scruples distract me, but at Church I had hopes to conquer them.

I bore abstinence this day not well, being at night insupportably heavy, but as fasting does not produce sleepiness I had perhaps rested ill the night before. I prayed in my study for the day, and prayed again in my chamber. I went to bed very early, before eleven.

After Church I selected collects for the Sacrament.

Finding myself upon recollection very ignorant of Religion, I formed a purpose of studying it.

I went down, and sat below, but was too heavy to converse.

*

This meditation of 1770 is written from painful experience:

JUNE 1, 1770. Every man naturally persuades himself that he can keep his resolutions, nor is he convinced of his imbecility but by length of time and frequency of experiment. This opinion of our own constancy is so prevalent, that we always despise him who suffers his general and settled purpose to be overpowered by an occasional desire. They, therefore, whom frequent failures have made desperate, cease to form resolutions; and they who are become cunning, do not tell them. Those who do not make them are very few, but of their effect little is perceived; for scarcely any man persists in a course of life planned by choice, but as he is restrained from deviation by some external power. He who may live as he will, seldom lives long in the observation of his own rules.

Boswell writes of him in 1771:

In his religious record of this year we observe that he was better than usual, both in body and mind, and better satisfied with the regularity of his conduct. But he is still 'trying his ways' too rigorously. He charges himself with not rising early enough; yet he mentions what was surely a sufficient excuse for this. 'One great hindrance is want of rest; my nocturnal complaints grow less troublesome towards morning; and I am tempted to repair the deficiencies of the night.' Alas! how hard would it be, if this indulgence were to be imputed to a sick man as a crime. In his retrospect on the following Easter-eve, he says, 'When I review the last year, I am able to recollect so little done, that shame and sorrow, though perhaps too weakly, come upon me.' Had he been judging of any one else in the same circumstances, how clear would he have been on the favourable side.

*

Johnson had a fine appreciation of human weakness – and this sermon is a devastating attack on a comfortable assurance that tomorrow will give ample time for repentance:

. . . That death is certain, every one knows; nor is it less known, that life is destroyed at all ages, by a thousand causes; that the strong and the vigorous are liable to diseases, and that caution and temperance afford no security against the final stroke. Yet as the thought of dissolution is dreadful, we do not willingly admit it; the desire of life is connected with anima- tion; every living being shrinks from his destruction; to wish, and to hope, are never far asunder; as we wish for a long life, we hope that our wishes will be granted, and what we hope, we either believe, or do not examine. So tenaciously does our credulity lay hold of life, that it is rare to find any man so old, as not to expect an addition to his years, or so far wasted and enfeebled with disease, as not to flatter himself with hopes of recovery.

To those, who procrastinate amendment, in hopes of better opportunities in future time, it is too often vainly urged by the preacher, and vainly suggested by a thousand examples, that the hour of death is uncertain. This, which ought to be the cause of their terror, is the ground of their hope; that as death is uncertain, it may be distant. This uncertainty is, in effect, the great support of the whole system of life. The man who died yesterday, had purchased an estate, to which he intended some time to retire; or built a house, which he was hereafter to inhabit; and planted gardens and groves, that, in a certain number of years, were to supply delicacies to his feasts, and shades to his meditations. He is snatched away, and has left his designs and his labours to others.

As men please themselves with felicities to be enjoyed, in the days of leisure and retreat; so among these felicities, it is not uncommon to design a reformation of life, and a course of piety. Among the more enlightened and judicious part of mankind, there are many who live in a continual disapprobation of their own conduct, who know, that they do every day what they ought to leave undone, and every day leave undone what they ought to do; and who therefore consider themselves, as living under the divine displeasure, in a state, in which it would be very dangerous to die. Such men answer the reproaches of conscience, with promises of amendment, promises made with sincerity and intention of performance, but which they consider, as debts to be discharged at some remote time. They neither sin with stupid negligence, nor with impious defiance, of the divine laws; they fear the punishments denounced against sin, but pacify their anxiety, with possibilities of repentance, and with a plan of life to be led, according to the strict precepts of religion, and to be closed at last, by a death softened by holy consolations. Projects of future piety are perhaps not less common, than of future pleasure, and are, as there is reason to fear, not less commonly interrupted; with this dreadful difference, that he who misses his intended pleasure, escapes a disappointment, but he who is cut off before the season of repentance, is exposed to the vengeance of an angry God.

Whoever has been deluded by this infatuation, and has hitherto neglected those duties which he intends some time to perform, is admonished, by all the principles of prudence, and all the course of nature, to consider, how much he ventures, and with how little probability in his favour. The continuance of life, though, like all other things, adjusted by Providence, may be properly considered by us casual; and wisdom always directs us, not to leave that to chance which may be made certain, and not to venture any thing upon chance which it will much hurt us to lose.

He who, accused by his conscience of habitual disobedience, defers his reformation, apparently leaves his soul in the power of chance. We are in full possession of the *present* moment; let the *present* moment be improved; let that, which must necessarily be done some time, be no longer neglected. Let us remember, that if our lot should fall otherwise than we suppose; if we are of the number of them, to whom length of life is not granted, we lose what can never be recovered, and what will never be recompensed, the mercy of God, and the joys of futurity.

That long life is not commonly granted, is sufficiently apparent; for life is called long, not as being, at its greatest length, of much duration, but as being longer than common. Since therefore the common condition of man is not to live long, we have no reason to conclude, that what happens to few will happen to us.

But, to abate our confidence in our own resolutions, it is to be remembered, that though we should arrive at the great year, destined for the change of life, it is by no means certain, that we shall effect what we have purposed. Age is shackled with infirmity and diseases. Immediate pain and present vexation will then do what amusement and gaiety did before, will enchain the attention, and occupy the thoughts, and leave little vacancy for the past or future. Whoever suffers great pain has no other care than to obtain ease; and if ease is for a time obtained, he values it too much, to lessen it by painful reflections.

Neither is an efficacious repentance so easy a work, as that we may be sure of performing it, at the time appointed by ourselves. The longer habits have been indulged, the more imperious they become; it is not by bidding them to be gone, that we can at once dismiss them; they may be suppressed and lie dormant for a time, and resume their force, at an unexpected moment, by some sudden temptation; they can be subdued only by continued caution and repeated conflicts.

The longer sin has been indulged, the more irksome will be the retrospect of life. So much uneasiness will be suffered, at the review of years spent in vicious enjoyment, that there is reason to fear, lest that delay, which began in the love of pleasure, will be continued for the fear of pain.

Neither is it certain, that the grace, without which no man can correct his own corruption, when it has been offered and refused, will be offered again; or that he who stopped his ears against the first call, will be vouchsafed a second. *He* cannot expect to be received among the servants of God, who will obey him only in his own time; for such presumption is, in some degree, a mockery of God . . . *(From a sermon on the text: 'Be not deceived, God is not mocked; for whatsoever a man soweth, that shall he reap'. Galatians vi.7)*

*

Despite past failures, Johnson renewed his resolutions in 1772:

EASTER EVE, APR. 18, 1772. I am now again preparing by Divine Mercy to commemorate the Death of my gracious Redeemer, and to form, as God shall enable me, resolutions and purposes of a better life.

When I review the last year, I am able to recollect so little done, that shame and sorrow, though perhaps too weakly, come upon me. Yet I have been generally free from local pain, and my strength has seemed gradually to increase. But my sleep has generally been unquiet, and I have not been able to rise early. My mind is unsettled and my memory confused. I have of late turned my thoughts with a very useless earnestness upon past incidents. I have yet got no command over my thoughts; an unpleasing incident is almost certain to hinder my rest. This is the remainder of my last illness. By sleepless or unquiet nights and short days, made short by late rising, the time passes away uncounted and unheeded. Life so spent is useless.

I hope to cast my time into some stated method.
To let no hour pass unemployed.
To rise by degrees more early in the morning.
To keep a Journal.

I have, I think, been less guilty of neglecting public worship than formerly. I have commonly on Sunday gone once to church, and if I have missed, have reproached my self.

I have exerted rather more activity of body. These dispositions I desire to improve.

I resolved, last Easter to read within the year the whole Bible, a very great part of which I had never looked upon. I read the Greek Testament without construing and this day concluded the Apocalypse. I think that no part was missed.

My purpose of reading the rest of the Bible was forgotten, till I took by chance the resolutions of last Easter in my hand.

I began it the first day of Lent, and for a time read with some regularity. I was then disturbed or seduced, but finished the old Testament last Thursday.

I hope to read the whole Bible once a year as long as I live.

Yesterday I fasted, as I have always, or commonly done, since the death of Tetty. The Fast was more painful than it has formerly been, which I imputed to some medicinal evacuations in the beginning of the week, and to a meal of cakes on the foregoing day. I can not now fast as formerly.

I devoted this week to the perusal of the Bible, and have done little secular business. I am this night easier than is customary on this anniversary, but am not sensibly enlightened.

*

In 1775, Johnson prepared his servant for his first Communion:

APR. 14 GOOD FRIDAY. Boswell came in, before I was up. We breakfasted. I only drank tea without milk or bread. We went to Church, saw Dr. Wetherell in the pew, and by his desire took him home with us. He did not go very soon, and Boswell stayed. Dilly and Miller called. Boswell and I went to Church, but came very late. We then took tea, by Boswell's desire, and I eat one bun, I think, that I might not seem to fast ostentatiously. Boswell sat with me till night; we had some serious talk. When he went I gave Francis some directions for preparation to communicate. Thus has passed hitherto this awful day.

10.30 pm

When I look back upon resoluti[ons] of improvement and amendments, which have year after year been made and broken, either by negligence, forgetfulness, vicious idleness, casual interruption, or morbid infirmity, when I find that so much of my life has stolen unprofitably away, and that I can descry by retrospection scarcely a few single days properly and vigorously employed, why do I yet try to resolve again? I try because Reformation is necessary and despair is criminal. I try in humble hope of the help of God. . . .

*

Boswell comments on Johnson's 'gross' enjoyment of food and wine. This very grossness led Johnson to pay much attention to fasting and even to give up wine for long periods. This was in his nature, which was always to struggle between his own rigid expectations of himself and his free, generous love of the good things of life. Boswell wrote of him:

Johnson, though he could be rigidly *abstemious*, was not a *temperate* man either in eating or drinking.

Johnson was especially careful about his food and fasting at Easter, although his unruly digestion, and a scrupulous examination of his motives, made it a difficult imposition.

1778, GOOD FRIDAY, APR. 17 . . . When we came home we had tea and I eat two buns, being somewhat uneasy with fasting, and not being alone. If I had not been observed I should probably have fasted.

*

Boswell recounts an incident which paints a striking picture of how seriously Johnson regarded his own sins.

To Mr. Henry White, a young clergyman, with whom he now formed an intimacy, he mentioned that he could not in general accuse himself of having been an undutiful son. 'Once, indeed,' said he, 'I was disobedient; I refused to attend my father to Uttoxeter market. Pride was the source of that refusal, and the remembrance of it was painful. A few years ago I desired to atone for this fault. I went to Uttoxeter in very bad weather, and stood for a considerable time bare-headed in the rain, on the spot where my father's stall used to stand. In contrition I stood, and I hope the penance was expiatory.'

*

The Doctor's diary for Easter 1779 is bleak:

EASTER EVE, APR. 3, 11 P.M. This is the time of my annual review, and annual resolution. The review is comfortless. Little done. Part of the life of Dryden, and the Life of Milton have been written; but my mind has neither been improved nor enlarged. I have read little, almost nothing, and I am not conscious that I have gained any good, or quitted any evil habit.

Of resolutions I have made so many with so little effect, that I am almost weary, but, by the Help of God, am not yet hopeless. Good resolutions must be made and kept. I am almost seventy years old, and have no time to lose. The distressful restlessness of my nights, makes it difficult to settle the course of my days. Something however let me do.

*

Old age never brought complacency to Johnson and he remained keenly aware of his faults to the end of his life. Boswell reports in 1780:

On his birth-day, Johnson has this note: 'I am now beginning the seventy-second year of my life, with more strength of body and greater vigour of mind than I think is common at that age.'

But still he complains of sleepless nights and idle days, and forgetfulness, or neglect of resolutions. He thus pathetically expresses himself:

'Surely I shall not spend my whole life with my own total disapprobation.'

CHAPTER 10

The Death of Dr Johnson

═══

Boswell writes of Johnson's death in 1784:

My readers are now, at last, to behold SAMUEL JOHNSON preparing himself for that doom, from which the most exalted powers afford no exemption to man. Death had always been to him an object of terror: so that, though by no means happy, he still clung to life with an eagerness at which many have wondered. At any time when he was ill, he was very much pleased to be told that he looked better. . . . Upon one occasion, when [someone] said to him that he saw health returning to his cheek, Johnson seized him by the hand and exclaimed, 'Sir, you are one of the kindest friends I ever had.'

His great fear of death, and the strange dark manner in which Sir John Hawkins imparts the uneasiness which he expressed on account of offences with which he charged himself, may give occasion to injurious suspicions, as if there had been something of more than ordinary criminality weighing upon his conscience. On that account, therefore, as well as from the regard to truth which he inculcated, I am to mention (with all possible respect and delicacy, however), that his conduct, after he came to London, and had associated with Savage and others, was not so strictly virtuous, in one respect, as when he was a younger man. It was well known that his amorous inclinations were uncommonly strong and impetuous. He owned to many of his friends, that he used to take women of the town to taverns, and hear them relate their history. In short, it must not be concealed, that like many other good and pious men, among whom we may place the apostle Paul upon his own authority, Johnson was not free from propensities which were ever 'warring against the law of his mind,' – and that in his combats with them, he was sometimes overcome.

Here let the profane and licentious pause: let them not thoughtlessly say that Johnson was an *hypocrite*, or that his *principles* were not firm, because his *practice* was not uniformly conformable to what he professed. . . . I heard Dr. Johnson once observe, 'There is something noble in publishing truth, though it condemns one's self.' And one who said in his presence, 'he had no notion of people being in earnest in their good professions, whose practice was not suitable to them,' was thus reprimanded by him: 'Sir, are you so grossly ignorant of human nature as not to know that a man may be very sincere in good principles, without having good practice?'

But let no man encourage or soothe himself in 'presumptuous sin,' from knowing that Johnson was sometimes hurried into indulgences which he thought criminal. I have exhibited this circumstance as a shade in so great a character, both from my sacred love of truth, and to show that he was not so weakly scrupulous as he has been represented by those who imagine that the sins, of which a deep sense was upon his mind, were merely such little venial trifles as pouring milk into his tea on Good Friday. His understanding will be defended by my statement, if his consistency of conduct be in some degree impaired. But what wise man would, for momentary gratifications, deliberately subject himself to suffer such uneasiness as we find was experienced by Johnson in reviewing his conduct as compared with his notion of the ethics of the Gospel? Let the following passages be kept in remembrance:

'O God, giver and preserver of all life, by whose power I was created, and by whose providence I am sustained, look down upon me with tenderness and mercy; grant that I may not have been created to be finally destroyed; that I may not be preserved to add wickedness to wickedness.'

'O Lord, let me not sink into total depravity; look down upon me, and rescue me at last from the captivity of sin.'

'Almighty and most merciful Father, who hast continued

my life from year to year, grant that by longer life I may become less desirous of sinful pleasures, and more careful of eternal happiness.'

'Let not my years be multiplied to increase my guilt; but as my age advances, let me become more pure in my thoughts, more regular in my desires, and more obedient to thy laws.'

'Forgive, O merciful Lord, whatever I have done contrary to thy laws. Give me such a sense of my wickedness as may produce true contrition and effectual repentance; so that when I shall be called into another state, I may be received among the sinners to whom sorrow and reformation have obtained pardon, for Jesus Christ's sake. Amen.'

Such was the distress of mind, such the penitence of Johnson, in his hours of privacy, and in his devout approaches to his Maker. His *sincerity*, therefore, must appear to every candid mind unquestionable.

It is of essential consequence to keep in view that there was in this excellent man's conduct no false principle of *commutation*, no *deliberate* indulgence in sin, in consideration of a counterbalance of duty. His offending and his repenting were distinct and separate: and when we consider his almost unexampled attention to truth, his inflexible integrity, his constant piety, who will dare to 'cast a stone at him'? Besides, let it never be forgotten that he cannot be charged with any offence indicating badness of *heart*, any thing dishonest, base, or malignant; but that, on the contrary, he was charitable in an extraordinary degree. . . .

I am conscious that this is the most difficult and dangerous part of my biographical work, and I cannot but be very anxious concerning it. I trust that I have got through it, preserving at once my regard to truth, – to my friend, – and to the interests of virtue and religion. Nor can I apprehend that more harm can ensue from the knowledge of the irregularities of Johnson, guarded as I have stated it, than from knowing that Addison and Parnell were intemperate in the use of wine; which he himself, in his Lives of those celebrated writers and pious men, has not forborne to record. . . .

He requested three things of Sir Joshua Reynolds: – To forgive him thirty pounds which he had borrowed of him; – to read the Bible; – and never to use his pencil on a Sunday. Sir Joshua readily acquiesced.

Indeed he showed the greatest anxiety for the religious improvement of his friends, to whom he discoursed of its infinite consequence. . . .

Johnson, with that native fortitude which, amidst all his bodily distress and mental sufferings, never forsook him, asked Dr. Brocklesby . . . to tell him plainly whether he could recover. 'Give me,' said he, 'a direct answer.' The doctor, having first asked him if he could bear the whole truth, which way soever it might lead, and being answered that he could, declared that, in his opinion, he could not recover without a miracle. 'Then,' said Johnson, 'I will take no more physic, not even my opiates; for I have prayed that I may render up my soul to God unclouded.' In this resolution he persevered, and, at the same time, used only the weakest kinds of sustenance. . . .

The Reverend Mr. Strahan has given me the agreeable assurance, that after being in much agitation, Johnson became quite composed, and continued so till his death. Having in his mind the true Christian scheme, at once rational and consolatory, uniting justice and mercy in Divinity, with the improvement of human nature, previous to receiving the Holy Sacrament in his apartment, he composed and fervently uttered this prayer:

'Almighty and most merciful Father, I am now as to human eyes it seems, about to commemorate for the last time, the death of Thy Son Jesus Christ, our Saviour and Redeemer. Grant, O Lord, that my whole hope and confidence, may be in His merits, and Thy mercy; enforce and accept my imperfect repentance; make this commemoration available to the confirmation of my faith, the establishment of my hope, and the enlargement of my charity; and make the death of Thy Son Jesus Christ effectual to my redemption. Have mercy upon me, and pardon the multitude of my offences. Bless my friends; have mercy upon all men. Support me by Thy Holy Spirit, in the days of weakness, and at the hour of death; and receive me, at my death, to everlasting happiness, for the sake of Jesus Christ. Amen.'

Having made his will on the 8th and 9th of December and settled all his worldly affairs, he languished till Monday, the 13th of that month, when he expired, about seven o'clock in the evening, with so little apparent pain, that his attendants hardly perceived when his dissolution took place.

CHAPTER 11

Occasional Prayers

========

Here are a few of the prayers which Johnson himself was persuaded to prepare for publication. Boswell introduces the first:

In 1750 he came forth in the character for which he was eminently qualified, a majestic teacher of moral and religious wisdom. The vehicle which he chose was that of a periodical paper [*The Rambler*]. . . . With what devout and conscientious sentiments this paper was undertaken, is evidenced by the following prayer, which he composed and offered up on the occasion: –

'Almighty God, the giver of all good things, without whose help all labour is ineffectual, and without whose grace all wisdom is folly: grant, I beseech Thee, that in this undertaking Thy Holy Spirit may not be withheld from me, but that I may promote Thy glory, and the salvation of myself and others: grant this, O Lord, for the sake of Thy Son, Jesus Christ. Amen.'

BEFORE ANY NEW STUDY

NOVEMBER. Almighty God, in whose hands are all the powers of man; who givest understanding, and takest away; who, as it seemeth good unto Thee, enlightenest the thoughts of the simple, and darkenest the meditations of the wise, be present with me in my studies and enquiries.

Grant, O Lord, that I may not lavish away the life which Thou hast given me on useless trifles, nor waste it in vain searches after things which thou hast hidden from me.

Enable me, by thy Holy Spirit, so to shun sloth and negligence, that every day may discharge part of the task which Thou hast allotted me; and so further with thy help that labour which, without thy help, must be ineffectual, that I may obtain, in all my undertakings, such success as will most promote thy glory, and the salvation of my own soul, for the sake of Jesus Christ. Amen.

AFTER TIME NEGLIGENTLY AND UNPROFITABLY SPENT
NOVEMBER 19. O Lord, in whose hands are life and death, by whose power I am sustained, and by whose mercy I am spared, look down upon me with pity. Forgive me, that I have this day neglected the duty which thou hast assigned to it, and suffered the hours, of which I must give account, to pass away without any endeavour to accomplish thy will, or to promote, my own salvation. Make me to remember, O God, that every day is thy gift, and ought to be used according to thy command. Grant me, therefore, so to repent of my negligence, that I may obtain mercy from Thee, and pass the time which Thou shalt yet allow me, in diligent performance of thy commands, through Jesus Christ. Amen.

ON THE STUDY OF PHILOSOPHY, AS AN INSTRUMENT OF LIVING
JULY, 1755. O Lord, who hast ordained labour to be the lot of man, and seest the necessities of all thy creatures, bless my studies and endeavours; feed me with food convenient for me; and if it shall be thy good pleasure to intrust me with plenty, give me a compassionate heart, that I may be ready to relieve the wants of others; let neither poverty nor riches estrange my heart from Thee, but assist me with thy grace so to live as that I may die in thy favour, for the sake of Jesus Christ. Amen.

WHEN MY EYE WAS RESTORED TO ITS USE
FEBRUARY 15, 1756. Almighty God, who hast restored light to my eye, and enabled me to pursue again the studies which thou hast set before me; teach me, by the diminution of my sight, to remember that whatever I possess is thy gift, and by its recovery, to hope for thy mercy; and, O Lord, take not thy Holy Spirit from me; but grant that I may use thy bounties according to thy will, through Jesus Christ our Lord. Amen.

PRAYER ON STUDY OF RELIGION

Almighty God, our heavenly Father, without whose help, labour is useless, without whose light search is vain, invigorate my studies and direct my enquiries, that I may by due diligence and right discernment establish myself and others in thy holy Faith. Take not, O Lord, thy Holy Spirit from me, let not evil thoughts have dominion in my mind. Let me not linger in ignorance and doubt, but enlighten and support me for the sake of Jesus Christ our Lord. Amen.

BEFORE THE STUDY OF LAW

SEPT. 26, 1765. Almighty God, the Giver of wisdom, without whose help resolutions are vain, without whose blessing study is ineffectual, enable me, if it be thy will, to attain such knowledge as may qualify me to direct the doubtful, and instruct the ignorant, to prevent wrongs, and terminate contentions; and grant that I may use that knowledge which I shall attain, to thy glory and my own salvation, for Jesus Christ's sake, Amen.

A prayer for use before Holy Communion:

AT THE TABLE

Almighty God, by whose Mercy I am now permitted to commemorate my Redemption by our Lord Jesus Christ; grant that this awefull Remembrance may strengthen my Faith, enliven my Hope, and increase my Charity, that I may trust in Thee with my whole Heart, and do good according to my power. Grant me the help of thy holy Spirit, that I may do thy will with Diligence, and suffer it with humble Patience; so that when Thou shalt call me to Judgment, I may obtain Forgiveness, and Acceptance for the sake of Jesus Christ our Lord and Saviour. Amen.

AT DEPARTURE, OR AT HOME

Grant, I beseech Thee, merciful Lord, that the Designs of a new and better life, which by thy Grace I have now formed, may not pass away without effect. Incite, and enable me by

Almighty and most merciful Father
whose clemency... I now presume...
... implore after a life passed
... of carelessness and
in wickedness, have mercy for mercy upon
my one—I have committed many
I have neglected many duties. I have done
what Thou hast forbidden, and left
undone what Thou hast commanded
Forgive, merciful Lord my sins my
negligences, and ignorances, and enable me
by thy holy Spirit to amend my life
according to thy holy word for Jesus
Christ's sake—Amen

Facsimile of a prayer by Johnson, ?1771

thy Holy Spirit to improve the time which Thou shalt grant me; to avoid all evil thoughts, Words, and Actions, and to do all the Duties which thou shalt set before me. Hear my Prayer, O Lord, for the sake of Jesus Christ. Amen.

*

Boswell records the following conversation which took place a few months before Johnson's death:

On Friday, June 11, we talked at breakfast of forms of prayer. JOHNSON: 'I know of no good prayers but those in the Book of Common Prayer.' DR. ADAMS (in a very earnest manner): 'I wish, Sir, you would compose some family prayers.' JOHNSON: 'I will not compose prayers for you, Sir, because you can do it for yourself. But I have thought of getting together all the books of prayers which I could, selecting those which should appear to me the best, putting out some, inserting others, adding some prayers of my own, and pre-fixing a discourse on prayer.' We all now gathered about him, and two or three of us at a time joined in pressing him to execute this plan. He seemed to be a little displeased at the manner of our importunity, and in great agitation called out, 'Do not talk thus of what is so awful. I know not what time GOD will allow me in this world. There are many things which I wish to do.' Some of us persisted, and Dr. Adams said, 'I never was more serious about any thing in my life.' JOHNSON: 'Let me alone – let me alone – I am overpowered.' And then he put his hands before his face, and reclined for some time upon the table.

In fact, of course, he did accede to the request and edited many of his prayers. He gave them, before his death, to his friend, the Revd George Strahan, who made further alterations and removed things which he felt were discreditable to the Doctor. The first edition appeared in 1785 under the title Prayers and Meditations.

Sources and Bibliography

SAMUEL JOHNSON

Early Biographical Writings, ed. J.D. Fleeman (Gregg International, 1973)

Diaries, Prayers and Annals, ed. E.L. McAdam Jr, with Donald and Mary Hyde (New Haven, CT, Yale University Press, 1959)

Review of Soame Jenyns' A Free Enquiry into the Nature and Origin of Evil, published in *The Literary Magazine: or, Universal Review* (May, June and July 1757)

Rasselas, ed. R.W. Chapman (Oxford University Press, 1927)

Rasselas, ed. D.J. Enright (Penguin, 1976)

The Idler (2 vols), 3rd edn (London, 1767)

The Idler and The Adventurer, ed. Walter J. Bate etc. (New Haven, CT, Yale University Press, 1963)

Sermons, ed. Jean H. Hagstrum and James Gray (New Haven, CT, Yale University Press, 1978)

Lives of the Poets, ed. Mrs Alexander Napier (G. Bell & Sons, London, 1913)

Letters: with Mrs Thrale's Genuine Letters to Him, ed. R.W. Chapman (Oxford University Press, 1984)

JAMES BOSWELL

Everybody's Boswell, ed. Frank Morley (G. Bell & Sons, London, 1930): an abridged edition of his *Life of Samuel Johnson* (1791) and *Journal of a Tour of the Hebrides with Samuel Johnson*, LLD (1785)

Journal of a Tour to the Hebrides (Penguin, 1984)

MRS THRALE

Anecdotes of the Late Samuel Johnson, ed. H.L. Piozzi (T. Cadell, London, 1786)

Editor's note: As far as possible, the texts are accurate, but I have made some small modernizations to Johnson's spelling and punctuation.